Sermon Tidbits

For information address:
J2B Publishing LLC
4251 Columbia Park Road
Pomfret, MD 20675
www.J2BLLC.com

Printed and bound in the United States of America.

This book is set in Garamond.

ISBN: 978-1-948747-61-5

Sermon Tidbits

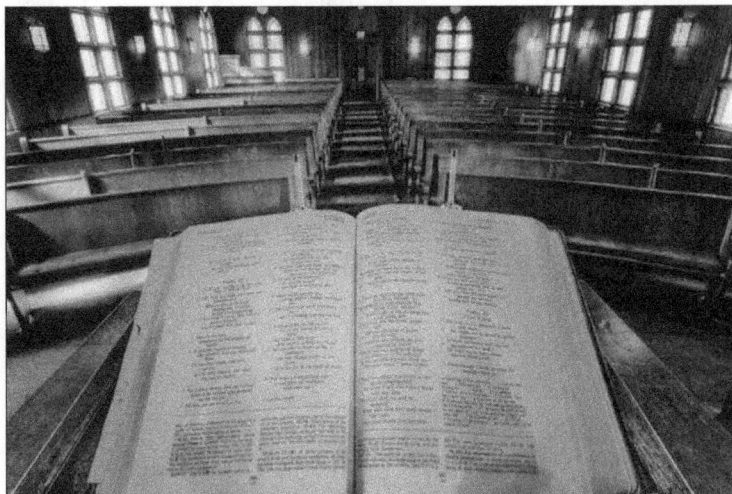

Randy Heddings

J2B PUBLISHING

Contents

INTRODUCTION   V

1– BAPTISMS AND GROWTH   1

2 - BEING GENUINE (MARK 11:11-22)   17

3 - BLESSING OR CURSE?   25

4 - CARNALITY IN THE CHURCH   31

5 - CONTEMPORARY VIEWPOINT TO THE BOOK OF RUTH37

6 - CREATION OF THE FAMILY UNIT   45

7 - AN EVERLASTING FELLOWSHIP!   57

8 - IT IS WELL! - GENESIS 50   69

9 - MINISTRY, NEAR AND FAR   75

10 - MY GREATEST CALLING   83

11 - ORDER OF SERVICE FOR A BELIEVER'S FUNERAL   105

12 - PAUL'S THORN IN THE FLESH   111

13 - SELECTING LEADERS - ACTS 6   119

14 - THE CROSS MAKES US VULNERABLE   129

15 - THE SICK SHALL BE HEALED   139

16 - SIGNS OF MAN'S CHURCH VERSUS GOD'S CHURCH147

17 - THE TRUTH ABOUT ABORTION   157

18 - WALK OF TRANSFORMATION   167

19 - WE'VE GOT WORK TO DO!   173

20 - INTEGRITY - MISSING INGREDIENT IN WALKING WITH
GOD   179

MEET THE AUTHOR   184

Introduction

Randy and Cheryl Heddings are the founders of Job's Place Ministries, a ministry dedicated to helping heal pastors who, after being attacked and mauled by their congregations for preaching the truth, feel like Job. Randy and Cheryl know how these pastors feel and understand the importance of their healing as they have been instrumental in 35 church plants across Texas and Mississippi.

Randy was raised in a religious home, so he had a good religious foundation already when he was saved at a revival service in a small Baptist Church in Prichard, Al. It was in June 1974 and Evangelist Sammy Hall was ministering. Shortly thereafter he was called to be a minister of the Gospel of Jesus Christ but resisted the call. He finally surrendered to preach with a provision God allow him to raise his children first. Twenty-five years later (1999) Randy, Cheryl and their 12-year-old daughter left Pascagoula, MS for an Associate pastor's position in central Texas. They were determined to share the Good News of our Savior, Jesus, and do as He instructed by making Disciples of His people.

By the end of that year, he was the pastor of a church in Missouri. In May 2001, Randy, Cheryl, and their daughter were sent to the mission field of Comanche, TX as church planters. It was there Randy learned his

Theology education was only an introductory course for the "Kneelology" education he received on the front lines of spiritual warfare. "Kneelology transformed his beliefs on ministry and the church. Two years later, the Lord sent them back into the pastorate and later to Evangelism.

After 20 years of preaching the Gospel, planting churches, and helping pastors heal, Randy felt there was value in preserving some of the message the Lord led him to deliver and passing on insights gained during their work for the Lord. As a result, the sermons contained in this work are for edification of the Body of Christ as encouraged in Eph 4:111-12.

Eph 4:11-12: *[11] And He Himself gave some to be apostles, some prophets, some evangelists, and some pastors and teachers, [12] for the equipping of the saints for the work of ministry, for the edifying of the body of Christ,*

The ministry illustrations given in these sermon tidbits are events experienced by Randy and Cheryl that God used them to teach and lead them towards more effective ministry. While you cannot quote them as having happened to you, God has shown he can use them in your message to provide insights to your congregation. Randy encourages you to use any of these messages as the Lord would lead with one caution. Most of these messages were delivered to Ministers and some of this material would appear harsh to congregations if delivered in the wrong spirit.

That said, it is with delight we share this information with you! Please enjoy it, cull through it, glean from it, and let the Holy Spirit be the umpire of your heart and guide you in your speech. We pray it encourages you and assists you in growing in grace with God.

1– Baptisms and Growth

Preparation: You will need four T-shirts; One adult black, two adult white, and one child white. Place the white child T-shirt inside the black adult T-shirt. Fold the two adult white T-shirts and the black/white combination T-shirt and place on a table near the lectern. You will also need rubber gloves and two buckets of water; one with just water, the other containing water and a blue dye.

Romans 6: 3-5: *"3Know ye not, that so many of us as were <u>baptized into Jesus Christ were baptized into his death</u>? 4Therefore we are buried with him by baptism into death: that like as Christ was raised up from the dead by the glory of the Father, even so we also should walk in newness of life. 5For if we have been planted together in the likeness of his death, we shall be also in the likeness of his resurrection."*

A significant outward expression of what God has done inside a believer is for them to follow the example of Christ in water baptism. Baptists observe Baptism as an Ordinance of the Church, but baptism is not a new ordinance.

1

THE ORDINANCE OF BAPTISM

The text of Hebrews 6: 1-2, speaks of "baptisms" (plural) which has a greater scope than the baptism we normally practice. According to the author of Hebrews, there is more than one type of baptism in scripture.

Hebrews 6:1-2: *1Therefore leaving the principles of the doctrine of Christ, let us go on unto perfection; not laying again the foundation of repentance from dead works, and of faith toward God, 2Of the doctrine of <u>baptisms</u>, and of laying on of hands, and of resurrection of the dead, and of eternal judgment."*

These baptisms are:

1. The baptism of creation to life - Genesis 1 & 7; 2 Peter 3: 6-7 (Reference Only)

2 Peter 3:6-7: *6Whereby the world that then was, <u>being overflowed with water</u>, perished: 7But the heavens and the earth, which are now, by the same word are kept in store, reserved unto fire against the day of judgment and perdition of ungodly men."*

2. The baptism of Moses from Egypt - Exodus 14:19-31; 1 Corinthians 10: 1-4 (Reference Only)

1 Corinthians 10:1-4: *1Moreover, brethren, I would not that ye should be ignorant, how that all our fathers were under the cloud, and all passed through the sea; 2And were all baptized unto Moses* *in the cloud and in the sea;* *³And did all eat the same spiritual meat;* *⁴And did all drink the same spiritual drink: for they drank of that spiritual Rock that followed them: and that Rock was Christ."*

3. The baptism of Ritual Cleansing - Leviticus 8: 5-9; Numbers 8: 6-7; 19:13, 20 (Reference Only)

Leviticus 8:5-9: *⁵And Moses said unto the congregation, This is the thing which the LORD commanded to be done.* *<u>⁶And Moses brought Aaron and his sons and washed them with water</u>. ⁷And he put upon him the coat, and girded him with the girdle, and clothed him with the robe, and put the ephod upon him, and he girded him with the curious girdle of the ephod, and bound it unto him therewith. ⁸And he put the breastplate upon him: also, he put in the breastplate the Urim and the Thummim. ⁹And he put the mitre upon his head; also, upon the mitre, even upon his forefront, did he put the golden plate, the holy crown; as the LORD commanded Moses."*

> **Step 1.** Pick up the black T-shirt combination, unfold it (make sure white T-shirt is still hidden inside) and show it to congregation. Ask them the color of the shirt. They say "Black." You explain it is really a colorless shirt as the fibers were colorless when woven. It appears black as it has been dyed black during manufacturer. This represents our present corrupt condition due to the natural sin of mankind.

3

Step 2. Spiritual awakening happens as we are shaken by the Holy Spirit. Hold the colorless/black T-shirt by the shoulder corners and shake the shirt. Let the colorless/white shirt work its way down from inside the larger shirt and come out the bottom. This signifies the rebirth of the repentant sinner. Speak to the qualities of the colorless/white shirt. Colorless/white, pure, without blemish, and smaller than the adult shirt because in rebirth we are babes in Christ.

Set the colorless/black adult shirt off to the side representing the death of the old man. Set the smaller colorless/white shirt beside it showing the new man.

4. The baptism of John unto repentance - Matthew 3: 1-6 (The Walk into life with Christ)

Step 3: Pick up a colorless/white adult shirt from tabletop. Explain it is dry and represents a convicted and repentant person.

"Regeneration, or the new birth, is a work of God's grace whereby believers become new creatures in Christ Jesus. It is a change of heart wrought by the Holy Spirit through conviction of sin, to which the sinner responds in repentance toward God and faith in the Lord Jesus Christ. Repentance and faith are inseparable experiences of grace. Repentance is a genuine turning from sin toward God. Faith is the acceptance of Jesus Christ and commitment of the entire personality to Him as Lord and Savior."

"Justification is God's gracious and full acquittal, based upon His righteousness, of any sinner who repents and believes in Christ. Justification brings the believer into a relationship of peace and favor with God."

Matthew 3:1-6:   *¹In those days came John the Baptist, preaching in the wilderness of Judaea, ²And saying, Repent ye: for the kingdom of heaven is at hand. ³For this is he that was spoken of by the prophet Esaias, saying, "The voice of one crying in the wilderness, Prepare ye the way of the LORD, make his paths straight." ⁴And the same John had his raiment of camel's hair, and a leathern girdle about his loins; and his meat was locusts and wild honey. ⁵Then went out to him Jerusalem, and all Judaea, and all the region round about Jordan, ⁶And were baptized of him in Jordan, confessing their sins."*

John's baptism was a symbolic, public baptism signifying a person's repentance (turning away) of their old lifestyle (way of thinking, previous actions) and their acknowledgment that God was to be obeyed in all things. Bear in mind, the Jewish people all believed **in** God and in the Holy Spirit. After Jesus' resurrection, it was believing **on** Jesus as the Christ they were having trouble accepting. To believe on Jesus requires a transition in thought and belief. The scriptures refer to believing in Jesus and believing on Jesus.

> **Illustration:** We have a small riding mower which we transport in the back of our pick-up truck. We get it into the truck with a set of aluminum ramps that fold in the center. The ramps are rated for a weight far greater than the weight of the mower and me. Before I drove up the ramp with the lawnmower, I believed **"in"** the ability of the ramps to hold our weight, based upon the instruction manual. As I drove up the ramps and our entire weight was supported by the ramps, my thoughts transitioned from believing **"in"** the ramps to believing **"on"** the ramps. My whole being, my safety, my welfare existed on whether those ramps could do their job. When we follow Jesus, we move from believing **"in"** Him to believing **"on"** Him. Jesus is capable and willing to place our every part of being on him to carry through this life and into eternity.

5. The baptism of Y'shua into His Body - Romans 6:3-5 (a continuation of John's Baptism)

> **Step 4:** The person has been led towards baptism by the word of God and gets baptized. Dunk the shirt into the water and pull it out quickly in the same manner as baptism. Explain the shirt is still colorless,

but now wet which represents the born-again believer, in obedience, being water baptized. They go in dry, come out wet but, aside from being wet, no other change. Place shirt on table next to the child's colorless/white shirt.

Romans 6:3-5: *³Know ye not, that so many of us as were baptized into Jesus Christ were baptized into his death? ⁴Therefore we are buried with him by baptism into death: that like as Christ was raised up from the dead by the glory of the Father, even so we also should walk in newness of life. ⁵For if we have been planted together in the likeness of his death, we shall be also in the likeness of his resurrection"*

Baptism is an outward expression of an inward work.

"Christian baptism is the immersion of a believer in water in the name of the Father, the Son, and the Holy Spirit. It is an act of obedience symbolizing the believer's faith in a crucified, buried, and risen Savior, the believer's death to sin, the burial of the old life, and the resurrection to walk in newness of life in Christ Jesus. It is a testimony to his faith in the final resurrection of the dead."

Water baptism is derived from two Greek words:

- Bapto: to cover wholly with a fluid or dip.

- Baptizo: to immerse or submerge. It is not the same as Bapto. In Hebrew, it is referred to as a Mikveh - an immersion. Basically, it is an immersion into another substance, for the purpose of being saturated by it, such as water.

6. The baptism in the Spirit of God for ministry - Matthew 3:11 & Luke 3:16 (God using You)

> **Step 5:** Pick up the other colorless/white adult shirt. Explain again the colorlessness of the shirt, the regeneration, the walk of obedience, and stepping into the life of surrender. Place the shirt into the bucket containing blue dye. Using a stick, move the shirt around in a manner to saturate every part of the colorless shirt. Explain how sanctification works on us from the inside out. Illustrate how we begin to change in our look and begin to look more like the image of God as we are transformed into His image of us.

Matthew 3:11: I indeed baptize you with water unto repentance. but he that cometh after me is mightier than I, whose shoes I am not worthy to bear: he shall baptize you with the Holy Ghost, and with fire:

Luke 3:16: John answered, saying unto them all, I indeed baptize you with water; but one mightier than I cometh, the latchet of whose shoes I am not worthy to unloose: he shall baptize you with the Holy Ghost and with fire:

"<u>Sanctification</u> is the experience, beginning in regeneration, by which the believer is set apart to God's purposes, and is enabled to progress toward moral and spiritual perfection through the presence and power of the Holy Spirit dwelling in him. Growth in grace should continue throughout the regenerated person's life."

The work of the Holy Spirit, as we grow in Christ, is to cleanse us from the inside out. The work began when He awakened (shook) us to be reconciled, through Jesus' work on the cross, to the Father by producing in us repentance and a desire to be obedient in baptism.

As the shaking goes on, Jesus is baptizing with the Holy Spirit as only He can do, and we are calmly cleansed. As you become saturated from the inside out, the Holy Spirit's cleansing removes all the impurities in your thoughts, words, and actions. You look more like Christ in nature and character and eventually become so much like Christ, the two of you cannot be separated. It is a permanent relationship.

> **Step 6:** Remove shirt and carefully wring out the water with dye. (Be sure to wear rubber gloves for this) Show the blue colored shirt to the congregation. This shirt shows the change God makes in us as we are sanctified. Explain, that the shirt is still colorless however, the dye is blue. The dye has

saturated the fibers of the colorless shirt so much that you can no longer see the colorlessness of the shirt. You can only see the change agent (blue dye). The shirt is still colorless; however, because of the saturation of the dye, you cannot separate the two. This is what happens with the Holy Spirit inside us. Place the colorless/blue shirt nest to the other shirts on the table.

The word Baptizo is used here, but in referring to the new covenant it presents the immersion of a believer "in the Spirit of God" and also "with Fire" (Matthew 3:11).

7. The baptism of fire for purification - Matthew 3:11 & Luke 3:16; 1 Peter 4:12-16 (Your life in Christ walked out)

1 Peter 4:12-16: *[12]Beloved, think it not strange concerning the fiery trial which is to try you, as though some strange thing happened unto you: [13]But rejoice, inasmuch as ye are partakers of Christ's sufferings; that, when his glory shall be revealed, ye may be glad also with exceeding joy. [14]If ye be reproached for the name of Christ, happy are ye; for the spirit of glory and of God resteth upon you: on their part he is evil spoken of, but on your part, he is glorified. [15]But let none of you suffer as a murderer, or as a thief, or as an evildoer, or as a busybody in other men's matters. [16]Yet if any man suffer as a Christian, let him not be ashamed; but let him glorify God on this behalf.*

The baptism of fire seems to come in the form of opposition from people around us. Many times we feel the fire when resistance is strong, and things don't seem to go our way.

> **Illustration:** The first church we pastored in the Ozark Mountains of Missouri was small. Within months of our arrival, attendance had grown to over 120. The small group who had run the church for decades said they wanted to grow, but in reality, they didn't. As the church grew, we were attacked as a family. After one rough evening with them, I spent several hours in prayer asking God to get the devil off my back and tell me what I was doing wrong. As the prayer line opened and things became clear, the Lord began to speak with me and took me to :
>
> ***Isaiah 48:10:*** *"Behold, I have refined thee, but not with silver; I have chosen thee in the furnace of affliction. 11 For mine own sake, even for mine own sake, will I do it: for how should my name be polluted? and I will not give my glory unto another."*

I was being baptized by fire in that refiner's fire. I was learning who owned the church, who ran the church, and what my place was within the church. I was learning that it wasn't all on me or about me; lessons that Bible College and Seminary could not teach.

You will often rehash events and ask yourself, "Why did I go through that and what purpose did it serve?" You may get answers, you may not. Some answers may take years to come. For example, in 2006, seven years after being at that church, we received one answer. While we were pastoring the church, a member received a call to serve in the ministry but did not answer that call then. A few years later he answered his call and had been pastoring a small church in the area for a couple years. It was obvious he had a pastoral call on his life, and he was phoning to ask if I would I make a trip to Missouri to be on his Ordination Council. I asked him, why, after seeing me in the worst place I had ever been, under the worst attack I had ever experienced, would he want me to be there during such a special time? He told me, he watched people attack me and my family relentlessly for months. He watched them team up against us and false accusations against us. He commented that during all that, I never quit loving them, I didn't preach anything judgmental or condemning, and only showed love and offered encouragement. He finished by saying, anybody that could withstand what we endured had something more in them than themselves. I was encouraged by this request and would have loved to attend, but the event conflicted with our youngest daughter's High School graduation and I declined.

It was not Randy, but the baptism Christ provides in the baptism of the Holy Spirit, the saturation of His very being, that allowed Randy to stand!

How do you get through the baptism of fire? Surrender to God and Praise Him! It is very easy to say and hard to do! The final reward on earth ends with rebirth into a secure place in eternity!

"Glorification is the culmination of salvation and is the final blessed and abiding state of the redeemed."

Looking at the four shirts explain:

- Colorless. yet black in sin

- Awakening (Kids colorless t-shirt, pure and without blemish)

- Conviction and repentance (Adult colorless t-shirt, pure and without blemish) Born-again believer

- Regeneration/Justification (Adult colorless t-shirt dipped in water) (Justified = Just/if/i/died) (Jesus died for me) (pure with the only change of being dunked)

- Sanctification (Adult colorless/blue t-shirt) (set apart for the work of God) (Pure with the righteousness of God showing through) Comes out changed to blue

Which of the three shirts represent you today?

God has more for you! He wants you so full of Him the things of this world cannot stand to be around you. He wants you to move beyond lack, sickness, loneliness, depression, heartbreak. Jesus said this: *"Fear not little flock for it is the Father's good pleasure to give you the Kingdom!"* You just need to walk right into it. It is worth everything you turn loose of for the greater gain you receive.

AMEN!

T-Shirt Object Lesson

This sermon uses T-shirts in an object lesson that is very effective in getting across the showing what happens at Baptism.

Preparation: You will need four T-shirts; One adult black, two adult white, and one child white. Place the white child T-shirt inside the black adult T-shirt. Fold the two adult white T-shirts and the black/white combination T-shirt and place on a table near the lectern. You will also need rubber gloves and two buckets of water; one with just water, the other containing water and a blue dye.

Step 1. Pick up the black T-shirt combination, unfold it (make sure white T-shirt is still hidden inside) and show it to congregation. Ask them the color of the shirt. They say "Black." You explain it is really a colorless shirt as the fibers were colorless when woven. It appears black as it has been dyed black during manufacturer. This represents our

14

present corrupt condition due to the natural sin of mankind.

Step 2. Spiritual awakening happens as we are shaken by the Holy Spirit. Hold the colorless/black T-shirt by the shoulder corners and shake the shirt. Let the colorless/white shirt work its way down from inside the larger shirt and come out the bottom. This signifies the rebirth of the repentant sinner. Speak to the qualities of the colorless/white shirt. Colorless/white, pure, without blemish, and smaller than the adult shirt because in rebirth we are babes in Christ.

Set the colorless/black adult shirt off to the side representing the death of the old man. Set the smaller colorless/white shirt beside it showing the new man.

Step 3: Pick up a colorless/white adult shirt from tabletop. Explain it is dry and represents a convicted and repentant person.

Step 4: The person has been led towards baptism by the word of God and get baptized. Dunk the shirt into the water and pull it out quickly in the same manner as baptism. Explain the shirt is still colorless, but now wet which represents the born-again believer, in obedience, being water baptized. They go in dry, come out wet but, aside from being wet, no other change. Place shirt on table next to the child's colorless/white shirt.

Step 5: Pick up the other colorless/white adult shirt. Explain again the colorlessness of the shirt, the regeneration, the walk of obedience, and stepping into the life of surrender and then place the shirt into the bucket containing blue dye. Using a stick, move the shirt around in a manner to saturate every part of the colorless shirt. Explain how sanctification works on us from the inside out. Illustrate how we begin to change in our look and begin to look more like the image of God as we ar6 transformed into His image of us.

Step 5: Remove shirt and carefully wring out the water with dye. (Be sure to wear rubber gloves for this) Show the blue colored shirt to the congregation. This shirt shows the change God makes in us as we are sanctified. Explain, that the shirt is still colorless however, the dye is blue. The dye has saturated the fibers of the colorless shirt so much that you can no longer see the colorlessness of the shirt. You can only see the change agent (blue dye). The shirt is still colorless; however, because of the saturation of the dye, you cannot separate the two. This is what happens with the Holy Spirit inside us. Place the colorless/blue shirt nest to the other shirts on the table.

2 - Being Genuine (Mark 11:11-22)

Mark 11:22: *"12 Now the next day, when they had come out from Bethany, He was hungry. 13 And seeing from afar a fig tree having leaves, He went to see if perhaps He would find something on it. When He came to it, He found nothing but leaves, for it was not the season for figs. 14 In response Jesus said to it, "Let no one eat fruit from you ever again."*

20 Now in the morning, as they passed by, they saw the fig tree dried up from the roots. 21 And Peter, remembering, said to Him, "Rabbi, look! The fig tree which You cursed has withered away."

22 So Jesus answered and said to them, "Have faith in God."

For years I struggled with the account of Jesus cursing the fig tree. A common explanation was that the tree represented a non-productive person that was supposedly serving the Lord. I never liked that analogy. One morning, after we had been in church planting for few years, I received and answer. While in prayer, I asked the Lord to explain the account of the fig tree. God had me read Mark 11:12 down to verse 22. It still didn't make sense. It just appeared that Jesus was on a rampage of anger after a bad night of sleep. Then the Lord took me back to verse 11 and showed me that Jesus had been in the Temple the night before and looked around. Jesus saw what was happening there and didn't like it then. He saw the corruption in the House of God, and it brought Him great displeasure. The next morning, Jesus and His disciples were heading back to Jerusalem for the day when they saw the fig tree.

The Lord Jesus, seeing the tree was in full bloom, went to it to see if it had any fruit on it. It didn't. Jesus already knew that because Jesus knows the growth of everything. Jesus is the vine, and we are the branches. Since we receive our nourishment from Him alone, He knows who will bear fruit and when.

God showed me that the fig tree represents the people of Israel and the country or governmental structure itself. This was represented best by the Temple. It stood for everything Israel was about. The Temple was operating at full capacity, was in full bloom, and giving every indication it would be bearing fruit in abundance. It was not bearing fruit at all. In fact, it was bearing false fruit (Psalm 1:3). The Priests of the Temple were teaching and following false teachings that were not from the wisdom of God but from the wisdom of man. Jesus went in and found the workers of the Temple dealing as Dove Handlers and Money Changers. They were practicing corruption within the House of God. They had begun to institute many things the Lord did not command. They were in a state that we would refer to in the church today as spiritual adultery. They had become extreme legalists with rules overriding God's Word. They were misleading the people of Israel and as a result they weren't capable of being productive as God's people. They had become caught up in religious tradition and dogma (Ezekiel 44:10-14). The destruction of the Temple in 70 AD corresponds to cursed fig tree.

My heart aches when we see people teaching others how to act like Christians, but they are not in a relationship with Christ themselves. We can teach people how to fit in when they come to church (Mark 7:8-13). It's easy to teach them to give a few dollars, to dress in a new way, or to attend church regularly. Lest you misunderstand, tithing is an act of worship, so we teach tithing. The result is a church filled with people who are following the rules, but not bearing fruit. They been in church for a long time but have no idea how to lead a person to the foot of the cross and help them into a personal relationship with Christ. Like Jews at the Temple, these people are not tapped into the living waters that never run dry (John 15:1-2). These people will dry up from the roots and die.

We should be careful in our teachings to let each person know that God loves His people and He alone is the source of true growth. He wants them to come to Him and abide in Him. Then He will allow fruit to bear in His season.

The fig tree simply represents the Temple and the fruit that the nation of Israel produced. Their nation was a product of the Temple. Are we a product of our churches? Are we like them or are we a product of the Holy Spirit? Jesus promises that when he comes to visit His Father's House today and finds things that are not in order, He will cleanse those Houses too! (Ezekiel 9:1-11)

How can this apply today with church plants? Could it be that we too get caught up in doing things our own way instead of God's way? It is easy to get caught up in the norm of things. People from all over will come in and look for programs within the church. There are many churches that are built from programs and man-made loyalties. It first takes a church to be grown before programs can be developed. How can we get caught up in this you might ask? There are things that happen to generate money to take care of the business of the church. Some churches have Bingo and others may have draw down raffles while others have bake sales. These things are sometimes done as an effort to build a church and we forget the focus is to bring Glory to God by leading souls to Him. There are other programs people begin to worship too! There is the requirement to have a school bus or van, we must have many youth activities and we must get a program to draw people in from all age groups. These programs can run us in circles for a long time. It is not bad to have programs within the church. Bake sale and other things that are not immoral or unethical are not bad either. The key thing is, we must not build the church on programs but rather have the church develop the programs that fit the church as it grows. These programs will shift from time to time and many of the programs will come and go. We should be careful that the programs of the church serve the people and the people don't become servants to the programs above God. With this, we should keep God as the main focal point of the work always! (John 12:32) Be careful about letting programs dictate the direction of the church just to keep up with the other churches in town. The fig tree was not cursed for being barren but for the falsity of the profession of being something it wasn't, symbolizing the people and the nation.

Jesus addressed the Scribes and Pharisees later during this same week. He called them hypocrites! He told them that they would go all over the sea and land to bring one person unto themselves and then make the person twice the son of perdition as they are. We are not trying to duplicate people as they serve the Lord but get the Good News out and see souls brought to God through Christ. Oh, the glory of watching the transformation of believers!

Jesus admonished the leaders then and reminds us now that the house of the Lord is to be a house of prayer. We must reverence His place as we come to worship Him. Jesus also said to bring no unclean vessel into the Temple. This is another thing we must be careful about. We must allow people to enter and hear the Good News, but the unclean, un-regenerated soul has no place in the leadership of the church. As believers, we must also enter God's presence pure in heart.

In verse 22, Jesus spoke to His disciples again and told them to have faith and believe in God. We are good at trying to do things for God when all that is required of us is to believe. We work to build churches and see the people come. He says that no man comes to the Father unless the Holy Spirit draws him. There really is nothing we can do that is more effective that fervent prayer for the lost. Jesus spoke in John saying that if He should be lifted up then He will draw all men nigh unto Him. God has placed the very best church growth plan before our very eyes. It doesn't entail spending or raising tons on money. God doesn't want His church to be encumbered with a load of debt! He simply wants us to believe that He will draw them and use us at the same time. When we bear fruit, we are lifting up the name of Jesus. God will send in the provisions to do the work that is going on with us.

It is no accident that the cursing of the fig tree is sandwiched between these two visits to the Temple and the ultimate cleansing of the Temple. God gave a revelation that I believe is as real today as it was then.

As we look back into Luke 2 and the account of the angels appearing to the shepherds as they watched their flocks by night, there is a picture of what God would have His church to look like. We see, as we read that the Angels came, and their singing was heard from the heavens. These angels were worshipping the Savior that was born that day. The modern church should be singing and praising God all the time! When we do this, we see the rest of the picture as God says, the Glory of God shown round about them. Brothers and Sisters, when we get to doing the things the way God wants them to be done, we get to where we can get our feet off the ground in praising Him, our knees on the ground when it comes to worship, and our face on the floor in prayer we will in fact see the Glory of the Lord shine round about the work. What a great feeling it is when all of this happens!

One day a severe storm passed over the area in central Texas where we were planting a church. When the storm was over, there was not one but two rainbows crossing the town. Cheryl and I were amazed to see two rainbows at the same time in the same area of the sky. It was beautiful. The next morning, a lady brought us a picture she had taken of one of the rainbows. The beginning of the rainbow appeared to be coming right out of the building we were using for church meetings. What an encouragement to us!

Here is an encouragement for you. It is often hard to believe that God will bring people who need Him to where He has placed us. But He does. We were in the middle of a Big Tent Revival in Texas. One morning a man showed up from 85 miles away. I asked him how he had heard about us and his response was that he didn't know we were there, but the Lord brought him right to us. God's Holy Spirit drew this man! This has happened to us more times than we can count. God's word and His promises are all we can stand on and know they will be exactly as God said they would be and will continue to be.

So, what do we do to accomplish the things that God would have us to do? We have found there is never enough prayer. I don't care how much you pray; you must pray some more. The work must be grounded on the Doctrine of Christ through God's Word and that alone. We will see the love grow as the knowledge of God's word increases (2 Peter 1:5-8). The more we learn about the Love of God, the more we realize it is all about God and His love for us, and nothing more. We must help to build a solid Biblical foundation as we go and provide proper Biblical spiritual guidance. When we do these things, Jesus will be lifted up! My prayer is that no rock will have to be dug up to praise the Lord on my account. May I always shout Glory and Honor to the Lamb that was slain!

3 - Blessing or Curse?

It is truly a great time for God's church as it is being readied for the bridegroom's return! There is much the LORD speaks about of what will transpire as the bride is readied!

Ruth is a great example of how we, as the church, are being prepared to receive the bridegroom when He returns to marry the bride! In the book of Ruth, a woman named Ruth was left to make her way. Every day she responsibly went out and worked hard in the fields, yet at the same time she was walking and working in the fields of an owner who covered her with grace and love. Her hard work and beauty attracted the owner's attention though, no doubt, she was dirty and sweating and smelling from that same hard work. As the favor of the field's owner grew and became known to Ruth and her mother, Ruth began to prepare for her bridegroom! She cleaned herself up, made herself look her best, and probably even smelled her best. However, being prepared for the bridegroom, did not prevent her from continuing to serve!

What would have me thinking in this direction? There are churches today that are teaching a feel-good gospel message that is failing to clean the Bride up and prepare her for the wedding! The real word is not being preached with power to break strongholds and demolish barriers that need to be destroyed. They are teaching religion and dogma as an escape, yet it is simply another form of bondage. Jesus said that men would hold to tradition and make the word of God no effect. Paul wrote to Timothy about teachers that will "tickle ears." Jeremiah wrote in Lamentation 2:14 that "Thy prophets" were seeing foolish things, failing to do the things God wants done, in paraphrased English.

They are not God's prophets; it has a direct link to what Paul wrote.

There are churches not teaching the fullness of God through the operation and purpose of Jesus, who is the Christ, the Holy Spirit from who we receive power and wisdom and are led, and the Loving heavenly Father. They are all we need to survive. God has given us everything to live successfully.

How can we do that and continue to see the things around us you may ask? Simple, we are not exempt, we are free and empowered! The word of God says no weapon formed against us will prosper but He never says they will not be formed or used against us. We simply must believe that they cannot be victorious in their attempts and attacks.

Then we have others that believe they have the only market on what God is doing and they can judge everything that comes their way with righteous judgment if they don't like it. These churches are different in that they can disperse anything to anybody, anyway they feel but once a Prophetic word comes to them, someone is speaking against them and what God is doing there. If the prophetic word begins to come to pass then, it is deemed as a curse that was spoken against the church and the person that spoke it is the devil himself.

So, we are looking at both ends of the spectrum here. We have a stagnant church that is existing without power and riddled with troubles in the lives of their people. Sickness is blamed for people's condition when an actual soul search and time with God would reveal that affliction is the issue. Everything that affects the church today is not from the devil, but much is part of the separation and cleaning up of the harvest.

Wait! We have power and signs in our church, and we operate in the 5-fold ministry. How can you say this about us? God is a God of order! He has specified order in His Word that keeps the church in harmony to what He wants them to learn. Discovering God's divine plan of order is a delicate balance because we are all people. We all strive for power, but it is the very act of submission that magnifies that power. No man is greater than another, even in the ministry.

I can say that I have received a prophetic word or two. I learned early to never discount that word right off but pray over that word and seek God. Some word I didn't like, nor did I want to accept them but, once spoken, if from God, it will come to pass!

Where am I going with this? John wrote in the Book of Revelation about the seven stars and seven candlesticks. It is explained that the seven stars represent the pastors of the seven churches represented by the candlesticks. As His revelation was given, the biggest revelation to me was that Jesus still was walking amid the churches, even in their times of troubles and turning away from the pure truth.

The same message that Jesus gave to those churches applies to the churches of the day. We must, as a body, repent and shed those things that are not of God. We must be willing to teach the truth, without apology and without fear. We must repent from prostituting the Gospel of the LORD for His people. We must turn away from the control factors that rule or lives and churches. We must change our mindsets and love people unconditionally, as Jesus does and as God does! We must repent from the tiptoe, weak kneed preaching trying to keep people comfortable in what they want to hear verses what the LORD would have them to hear. People are teaching there is no literal Hell, though the word of God makes it plain that Jesus himself went there to conquer the territory and take the keys! People are teaching there is no need for repentance once you have come to salvation, yet the word of God is plain about working out your own salvation with fear and trembling and crucifying the flesh daily. There are even folks that try to hedge in with a little philosophy about reincarnation. Of course, the big one today is that sex marriages are ok in the eyes of God. These are just a few things that we come against in the ministry that are being taught in local churches. If these things are being taught in a church, the church will not grow because lies do not bring life but rather death. These are some of the causes for the abomination of desolation to take place in the Holy place. The House of God is being desecrated for man's pleasure. These things must be cleansed before Jesus will return.

I believe in the next year, we will see a cleansing of the churches. True believers must show restraint as some people are dealt with by the LORD during this time. There will be those close to us we feel are being attack by the devil, but it will be the LORD refining them. We as a body of believers will have to trust God to receive Jesus bad to take out His bride without spot or blemish. We have to learn to trust God to do this work and not interfere, but LOVE people as they go through these things. Yes, Jesus will know us as He says we will know each other, by our Love!

Look for the shaking to come! God loves His creation, and He is allowing His plan to come forth. He is in control.

Hope can I be a blessing and be blessed? Easy, love people unconditionally! Give sacrificially to the LORD as you feel led by the Holy Spirit, not as instructed by man and let the world see Jesus in you and through you. Seek God in all you do!

How can I be a curse or be cursed? Hold to self and not change unless it helps me first. Reject people and reject God's leading in my life. Pile up my treasures on earth through personal greed.

Like Ruth, we must follow instruction that is sound, and we must continue to labor until the time is full and then, your redemption and the redemption of the church will come. There is much to learn from how Ruth operated before she was redeemed that will help us in getting ready for our time with Christ as a body and as individuals. Work, remain positive, be noticed because of your work and let God's Holy Spirit teach us all how to clean up our lives for the KING of Kings and LORD of Lords! When the harvest is complete and brought in, let us be also at the feet of our Savior!

So, what will it Be? Blessing or Curse?

4 - Carnality in the Church

Numbers 12:1-2; *"And Miriam and Aaron spake against Moses because of the Ethiopian woman whom he had married; for he had married and Ethiopian woman. And they said, Hath the Lord indeed spoken only by Moses? Hath he not spoken also by us? And the Lord heard it."*

As we read Old Testament writings, we find a small squabble about power within the organizational structure. God had selected Moses to speak directly to and through to His people. While they were out of the will of God, God referred to them as Moses' people. We see a position of jealousy coming into play. There was murmuring in the camp from Aaron and Miriam. They were upset about something. This sounds a lot like what we must deal with as church planters. There is someone that is going to come in and begin to tell you what the Lord is saying. I am not saying that God doesn't speak to them. This whole rumor started out as a smoke screen against Moses. Moses had married a Cushite woman (Numbers 12:1-2). This was an interracial marriage. His brother and sister began a revolt around the camp. They got people to talking about Moses, trying

31

to demean his position. They had used worldly things to try to change the focus of things. God says that Moses was "meek". This is a word that has been twisted and turned to mean that we should come to a position of compromise. There are churches full of compromise! God isn't looking for more of what already exists! God wants a genuine church centered on His Word and His Grace towards all people. It is not a free rodeo ride that we can get on and enjoy. Being a Christian entails a lifelong commitment to service and standing on the promises of God. God had told Moses what was going on and where He was leading them and Moses simply stood on those things, knowing God is indeed God. This is the approach we should take as we encounter challenges in the ministry as we move forward in faith. Being meek does not at all mean being weak but being strong on the word of God and not wavering, sticking to the path God places you on.

Moses' brother and sister were summoned to the Tabernacle to the first big tent revival ever. God met them at the door of the tent and spoke with them. He issued a stern warning to them. He told them that if there is a prophet among you, "I will speak to them in dreams and visions" but it wasn't so with Moses. God specifically stated that He would speak to Moses face to face, so that he could understand Him. Moses had a direct line to the Lord. Moses was the chosen leader, by the Lord, and that was the respect that God gave to him and required of His people in return.

I remember one night after prayer meeting; we were in the back of the church discussing things that needed to be done in the church. We had a person telling me that we needed to abandon certain plans the church had a vision for. They wanted to pull back all they were doing and center directly within the church and its four walls. That wasn't what the Lord was leading us to do. I told him that the Lord had told me certain things, which we discussed, and he returned with a loud tone, how would you know that? Well, I told him, it was quite simple, the Lord told me these things. That ended the discussion. God will reveal things to you that only you will know. It is your position to share that vision and watch God lead the way as you pray. I am not saying that others will not eventually come in with ways to reach that vision that will not match up with your thought pattern. The approach may be different but the vision the same in many cases.

We find Moses and his brother and sister at the tent. Miriam was stricken with leprosy and banished from the camp. That was her punishment which certainly meant death for her. God has issued a death sentence on to Moses' sister for her behavior. He got right to the root of the problem in dealing with this situation. God always knows where the source of the problem comes from and sometimes, we, as people, miss the exact place of origin. Aaron appealed to Moses and Moses pled to God for Miriam. God left her out of the camp for seven days but did not move the camp. Sometimes, we find ourselves standing on the outside of the camp and God stands in wait for us to get back in so He can move His kingdom on earth further towards the promised land.

Leprosy is a Biblical disease that causes separation. It touches all the senses of the human body. It will cause you to not feel, then later not smell or taste, eventually it will get your eyes and then into your hearing. Those that are trying to hinder the progress of God's work may be stricken with spiritual leprosy. They will reach a place where all they can feel is what they want to feel, all they can see is what they lust for, all they can hear are those things which please them, and all they can smell is odorless because they can no longer smell the stench of the devil in their nostrils. People no longer have the thirst for righteousness just the need to speak hurtful things against what the Lord is trying to do.

When you see this happening the church planter becomes the ready target. No senses equal spiritual death or separation from God until intercession or repentance is made. It is easier to get placed into a place of banishment than what we would ever care to believe.

God's judgment falls on some people every day as they walk the face of the earth. It is sad to see that these things happen however, it is from a different perspective, encouraging that we have a God who is committed to do the things He has told us He would do as He paves the way.

There will be those that will create problems, but God will handle them. You don't even have to say a word to anyone but Him. He knew before you did. I once got upset with a man for his comments in the church about scaring people into salvation. I listened to him yell at me for about an hour and finally just told him to go home and he should find another church. God chastised me and told me to go and make amends with him. I did and the man came back to the church. He didn't stay long, but when he left, the Lord told me I had done my part. It was during that time I learned that God takes people out when He gets ready. It is not up to me to separate the wheat and the tares for Him. It is merely my duty and calling to preach to all people the same. The separation of the wheat and the tares and the sheep from the goats is an ongoing process that will culminate at the rapture of the church.

Many times, I have seen the Lord sit still until someone that is essential to the work returns home from a wandering experience. I believe we all spend times in the wilderness at one time or another. Just be encouraged that God is the one leading you as you plant churches, and He is the one that will make the crocked places straight and break down the gates (Isaiah 45:1-3). He has the way already paved. All we need do is get aboard the Highway of Holiness and be on the fast track to His glory (Isaiah 35:8). The Bible says that He directs the footsteps of the righteous. There is another scripture in the Psalms where the Psalmist wrote the He is a lamp unto our feet and a light unto our path. There have been long periods of time that the Lord would only let me see one step at a time. Had He allowed me to see the pathway He had us on, I surely would have run from the way He wanted me to walk. Never in my lifetime could we have ever imagined planting one church let alone four and a distribution warehouse in twenty months with no money. Had God told me these things from the beginning, surly He would have had a fight with me going, like He didn't already! It was a great walk looking back from this side!

5 - Contemporary Viewpoint to the Book of Ruth

In the 1st chapter of the Book of Ruth, we find Elimelec moving his family out of Israel and into their own desert experience. There is nothing in scripture which says God led Elimelec out of Israel, yet history proves it was God's plan for this man to take his family into the land of Moab because Elimelec's individual action was part of God's divine plan for developing the lineage of Jesus Christ. You see, had he not taken his family to the desert, Ruth would never have come on the scene.

Some teach that Elimelec is taking his family out of the will of God and will allow that thought pattern to play out through the death of his two sons and his death as well. We must look at the meanings of his children's names since they are interpreted as "puny" and "sickly." It really seems that they were walking out their chosen path to their chosen destiny.

Naomi takes on the role of the Holy Spirit in this Book as we see the desire for her to return to her homeland. The two daughters in law were going to go back with her. She stopped at the edge of town, on the brink of major decision, a crisis decision time in the lives of these two women. She lays out the facts that life will forever change should they follow her. One, Orpah, decides she didn't want the change and walks of the pages and out of the Book, never to be heard from again, but Ruth says that she will sell out wholly to the leading, decisions and path of Naomi, regardless of the future. It was a right now, permanent decision for her. She gave up her everything. She gave up her land, her family, her gods and her future to follow the conviction and love she felt. Naomi, the type and shadow of the Holy Ghost, is now going to work on Ruth's behalf; we just don't see it for a while.

Naomi and Ruth return home worn out in the natural and empty in the spiritual. Nevertheless, they are now home. As the harvest season is in full swing when they arrive, Ruth, in her new life, goes out to work in the field. Ruth now represents the worker in the Kingdom of God and the church as well. She has a dual role as we see it unfold. It is not only personal but corporate. She is led, the Book says, she "happed" upon a field owned by Boaz. I am not one to believe too much on happenstance since the Bible says that God directs the footsteps of the righteous! She was drawn into that field through a divine connection! Remember, Naomi is the type and shadow of the Holy Ghost here. Boaz ends up with another key type and shadow role as well as the type and shadow Ruth is walking out.

Boaz owned the field Ruth was working in. Notice, a newly converted person, brought into a new place, is now working in the vineyard. Does this sound like a conversion experience and new-found relationship beginning to grow or what! Ruth is hard at work, she is toiling in the heat, the dust and dirt, hidden in the corners of the field. She is in obscure places, doing menial tasks but yet is noticed through this. The owner of the field sees her in her dedication and commitment. He seeks to find out who she is. He saw her in her beauty through her work. In case you haven't placed it together at this point, Boaz represents the Christ as the owner of the field and he sees his person and his church out laboring in the earth, in places of obscurity, in places of lack, in places of hardship but yet, sees the pureness of what they are doing. This is a personal commitment and corporate commitment issue for us as we serve the LORD through the church and in our lives. Ruth was not mumbling, groaning or complaining, simply working as hard as she possibly could.

Because of her willingness to do whatever it takes, Boaz, (a type and shadow of the Christ), tells his workers, (his angels), to allow her favor, to expand her territory and even bless her by dropping handfuls of grain on purpose. What a great thing! We see that dedication brings forth provision and blessing. We have yet to see where Ruth has said anything. When Ruth finally speaks it is with humility that the owner would speak to her. She was so well blessed that she was allowed to work the corners of the fields throughout both harvest times. She had indeed found favor with the master. When we find favor with the Master, He will allow for us to have double portions of Blessings, Double times in locations, Double everything! He owns it all, even the people.

Ruth, the student, the believer, the church, returns to Naomi, the Holy Ghost and tells her what has happened and how grateful she was. She had plenty of food as well. She was blessed for her hard and dedicated work. She wasn't working for herself either, she was working to help Naomi, the type and shadow of the Holy Ghost! At the point that Ruth explained this to Naomi, she was in turn told about how Boaz was kinsman to Naomi and subsequently to Ruth. Once the revelation was made that Boaz was the redeemer for her, in all likelihood, Naomi, the Holy Ghost began to prepare the Bride for marriage. Now we see the individual redemption and the redemption of the church or the marriage supper of the lamb as we often call it.

Naomi taught (a role of the Holy Ghost) Ruth about how to present herself for marriage to the Kinsman Redeemer. She was taught how to get cleaned up, dressed well and smelling nice. She was at her best. This process in the lives of people is not so easily done through the church. This is indeed a role of the Holy Ghost. It is the Holy Ghost that cleans us up and teaches us the things we must know to move to higher places in

God. Thank goodness for this picture in the Book of Ruth about the teaching and grooming process of mankind in preparation for the marriage of Christ to the Bride or the church. We know that Ruth was saved through her repentance in chapter 1, and since this is also a picture of the redeeming power of the Christ, it runs in two veins at the same time. Since the New Covenant hadn't been established yet, the person had to be literally bought out of bondage just as we had to be bought out of the bondage of sin with a perfect and acceptable sacrifice through God's only son. He had to be a willing sacrifice and be able to pay the price. We see these qualities in Boaz in the redemption of Ruth as well. We find that once Ruth was readied and sent to the threshing floor to be with Boaz, to sit at his table and dine with him, she continued to give obedient commitment to him (servanthood). She went to him and revealed to him that she knew who he was and that she needed to be redeemed and wanted him to do it. There was a small hindrance as there was another kinsman a little closer that had the first chance to redeem her. He told her to rest and let him work for her and he would take care of it. You know there is yet another person vying for your soul as well as the LORD. That one is the devil. He would like to be able to get you but yet, in all his evil, he cannot afford to do what is right in fear of his image. You will find this character trait played out in the nearer kinsman as he is described. He was told if he could redeem her, go ahead. He was called out publicly, before witnesses, but would not perform. The enemy only works in the cover of darkness. He will not do things in the open. He knows he cannot win. Once that was accomplished, the rights to Ruth were cast down by the nearer kinsman, Boaz sealed the deal with the enemy saying that he knows owns her, lock, stock and barrel. The enemy is concerned for the things of this world and nothing more. If it serves to make him look good, it is fine but if it is going to cause him a black eye, he won't mess with it. Jesus went to the Depths of the earth and took the keys of Hell and sealed our redemption defeating the enemy for us.

At one point, in the night, before the redemption action took place, Ruth laid at the feet of Boaz in an act of service to him. She got up early and left to return home before daylight. While she waited on the redeemer to work, she remained at his feet. How great to see a people that will remain at the feet of the Redeemer until His work is finished here on earth. How great to see a church and to have it stay at the feet of the Redeemer until He returns. How great to know we have a Redeemer who is working while we are resting!

When Ruth returned home, Naomi asked if she had been redeemed. While not in those exact words, that was her meaning! It was as if she had asked, have you received the riches of heaven for your seeking? It wasn't like she didn't know already.

We know through the last chapter that Ruth was redeemed by Boaz and they had a son. That son's name was Obed. Four generations later came a young man named David, who went on to be a great king of Israel. Once Ruth was redeemed, she was blessed, and her family was blessed after her. Once we get into a spiritual walk that pleases God, through the Redeemer Christ, we will also be blessed, our off-spring will be blessed and their off-spring will be blessed, as long as we hold in the way.

Once a church actually grabs on to the fullness of what God has done through our Redeemer Christ, we will see our spiritual off-spring become fruitful, live in abundance and have the blessing of watching new ministries and churches start that will be true believing churches, sold out and married to the Christ! We will see the Holy Ghost preparing the church for the return of the Bridegroom so that the final stage of redemption will take place in the lives of the believers and the church.

Yes, we have a Redeemer as shown through this Book of the Bible! We have a clearer picture of the redemption though as to how it applies to us as individuals and as a corporate body or the church. Yes, there are people living out these types and shadows in this text and yes there are those that will read for the dirt and garbage that is brought out through religion, but the truth is this:

1)	We have a Kinsman named Jesus that is ready, willing and able to redeem us

2)	We have a Holy Ghost teacher that grows us up in the ways of the LORD

3)	We have an individual walk with God through Christ

4)	We have a corporate (body) walk with Christ

5)	We must make a complete turn in our old ways to new ways (God's)

6)	We must be willing to labor anywhere, anytime, for any length of time

7)	We must remain content in what we do for the LORD and others

8)	We have a final redemption in the marriage supper of the Lamb

Process of salvation is simple:

1)	We are saved!

2)	We are being saved!

3)	We will be saved!

6 - Creation of the Family Unit

Genesis 1:27-28; *"So God created man in his own image, in the image of God created he him; male and female created he them. And God blessed them, and God said unto them, Be fruitful, and multiply and replenish the earth, and subdue it; and have dominion over the fish of the sea, and over the fowl of the air, and over every living thing that moveth upon the earth."*

It was God's intended purpose for the world to exist and do His work here on the earth as a family unit. God commanded the replenishment of the earth through propagation under the image of God. That image is characterized through the heart of Jesus as He ministered during His time here on earth.

God felt the importance of relationships with Him and fellow man, especially those that are family, be dealt with in love, compassion, mercy and forgiveness. These are just some of the attributes that Jesus displayed while He was with mankind. We find, as we look at the New Testament writings that God has brought a thread of family together as much as is humanly possible up until the time of the arrival of the Christ! We see the bloodline of Jesus being

45

brought out with Matthew's account of the genealogy of the Christ child. We find the adoption of Rahab into the family of God as the walls of Jericho were brought down because she believed what she had heard about the Father of the chosen people. The Father of all brought her right in. We find Tamar brought in because of her desire to have a child and caused Judah to do some things that he was later called to account for, and the offspring of Tamar end up in the genealogy of the Christ as well. We find Perez located within the account of Matthew. We find that Boaz was a man of great influence and stature in Bethlehem, and he redeemed Ruth, a Moabite woman, as her kinsman redeemer and 4 generations later, King David came from that bloodline. Ruth did not have to go through those generations of purging to be elevated into the Kingdom of God, just had to be redeemed. This is true of us all! We must believe that the work of Jesus on the cross paid the price for our sin! This being the case, God was working to reconcile the family unit through a renewed relationship with Him through His only begotten Son.

God felt so highly of His establishment of family order, that it is patterned after divine order, that in the intimacy of relationship new things were birthed. This is where we are introduced with the word "know" that we find throughout the entire writings of the scriptures. The word "know" does not insinuate that we are familiar with someone or something. I can say that I know President Bush but beyond the name, it really means nothing. This word has a meaning on intimacy. We will find some great things happen when we intimately know each other. It is then that we can be aware of the heartbeat of the person to whom you are related. Parents are to be regarded as "important" and "honored" in their place of the lives of their offspring. This deals with both a physical side and that of the spiritual side where your fruit produces (re)birth.

As Noah was "recovering" (for lack of a better word) after the flood, he drank of the wine of the vineyard. He became drunk. His son Ham saw him in his weakness and mistake and felt it his obligation to announce it publicly to his brothers, who went and respectfully covered their father. This was a blanket of course but so often, as children, we want to speak out against our parents and broadcast their frailties as opposed to covering them in a blanket of love. Ham's actions caused him to become cursed! This could not have been an isolated case as we read through the Bible but rather a pattern or God would not have addressed it in the "LAW" or "Ten Commandments" as we refer to them. There is much written about family and Parents in the Word of God!

Exodus 20:12; "Honor thy father and thy mother; that thy days may be long upon the land which the Lord thy God giveth thee."

This is the changing place for the relationship with God to the relationship with mankind. It is where our relationship changes from that of Vertical to that of Horizontal. It all begins with a parental relationship. Yes, children feel they can make it without their parents, and some go throughout life doing just that. There will always be a void in their relationships with their spouse and children that will trickle through life on earth. In order to understand the fullness of a relationship with the Father we must also have a strong relationship with our parents and others. If the parents will not let you close, do your part that is what you are accountable for.

God asks in the writings of John, how can a man love God whom he has not yet see yet hate his brother whom he can see? (1 John 4-20) I ask, in this time of the world, how can families be broken and shattered by its own family members lest there be a true relationship with the heavenly Father missing? I am convinced that one's relationship with their worldly family is a direct reflection of their true relationship with the Heavenly Father. God wants His children to have fellowship with Him, love on Him and tell Him so. He wants your help and mine too, in accomplishing His will on earth. He wants the family of God to be brought back together! He is not looking for the division that is taking place!

God wants families to love each other and encourage each other. He does not want Brothers to be against Brothers or Fathers against Sons, although He is not blind to this happening. Jesus spoke of these times as He gave what we know as the Olivette Discourse. It really seems that some family members thrive on the attention they can draw from causing a division. This division comes from many areas. It can come from envy, strife, jealousy, and covetousness. There are many areas that family members use to exploit other family members to isolate them from other family members and sorrowfully from their family members own children. Instead of encouraging others in the family to do that which is right, they encourage them to walk in a way that seems good to them leading them astray and causing further division. God simply cannot be happy with this type of treatment towards each other although He did identify it. As these things happen around you and to you, by relatives and those who call themselves Christian, I encourage you in saying that these are not God's plans and these people are not really serving the loving God that we are to know. The ultimate rest in Christ comes from knowing that God sees and knows all! These actions will not be unpunished. People all over are doing these things and destroying the family unit. Is it any wonder the family unit is losing ground in today's society? People that profess to be believers will not even uphold the family unit, as designed, until it doesn't meet something else they don't agree with and then they have the perfect understanding of the family unit. It is all about the god of self they are serving and not the God of All!

I would be so open as to let you know that while I was not walking right with God, my relationship with my parents was strained. I avoided them and would not speak openly with them about things going on. They always wanted to help but I pushed them aside. They wanted me more than I wanted them, but I needed them more than ever. This may be a place where you may be or know someone who is there. This was also the same place I was in my relationship with God during the same timeframe. I was not talking to God either and was, as foolish as it sounds, trying to avoid God too!

The commandment that God gives us in Exodus instructs us to honor our parents. We must honor and love our parents regardless of the situation. It is not really an option for us. If we do as God says this commandment comes with a promise! If we don't do these things, I believe we can expect the opposite to come to us. Honoring our parents doesn't stop as we get out of the house. I have found that it is a lifelong commitment that we decide to make, and we live with it, regardless of the way we may have to flex later. I use the word flex as opposed to sacrifice because we will not sacrifice. God told me once that He never gave us instruction without making first the provision! We have been able to walk this out in our life as well. The reason others may never walk it out is that they choose self over the will of God! There is no secret or really any argument about that. It is a lack of trust in God to do as He says He will do in providing all our need. We want to get all our need, all the other families need, and the entire world's need all without sacrifice or flexibility or really obedience. If a person can not give up a job to help one's parents or move across a nation or even drive a few miles out of their way, just how far do you truthfully think they will go for God when He speaks to them? Only as far as they desire. This is not true following. This is patronizing God! This is not following God but trying to serve God as we feel like serving God! Who do we really think we are fooling? Certainly not God, and surely, we too would know better! We cannot get wrapped around worldly things nor let worldly things keep us from heaven.

A year or so ago, the Lord spoke to me one night and told me the day was coming that I would have to place the family before the church and the church would understand. Within two weeks I was fully aware of what the Lord was speaking about. I am glad I heard the voice of God as He spoke to me! I was not caught by surprise by what was going on! I knew what was happening behind the scenes in this situation and what was going to be required of us from that point on. We did not hesitate to do as the LORD had said. Why? God ordained the family unit long before the church was manifested on earth. I am convinced, if we know the heartbeat of the Father in Heaven; we will be close to our own family (parents) and will know their heartbeat and will as well. We will do whatever it takes to carry forth the will of both the Heavenly Father we serve and the earthly father we honor.

There is a divine order for helping and assisting parents, especially widowed mothers. This order begins with the firstborn son and filters down from there. Today, it is a freewill thing and people hang their hat on the "freewill" they have! In the Old Testament, the option was, step up or die. Aren't we fortunate to live under the New Covenant of God's Grace? Many of us find excuses; we call them reasons, to sidestep our obligations to continue with our own lives regardless of what it costs others. We do what we call is convenient as opposed the will of the Father and father. We grab at scriptures and try to justify our reasoning by extracting such scriptures that support our desires but never want to entertain the ones that point out our responsibility. With this shed responsibility, we still carry the penalty for not doing what we are supposed to do. In some form or fashion, we will ultimately be accountable for these decisions and actions we make towards our parents and family members.

It is not all about us and parents; it is about parents as well. Parents should honor the role of parenthood in the lives of their children as well. Interfering with the raising of your children's children should be handled with godly wisdom and not personal feelings. What you feel may not be fair in dealing with a child may be exactly what that child needs that moment. I am not talking about abuse! Defining abuse is an area that is very tough to truly define! There are some legal interpretations under the laws, and we must be careful when dealing with our own children let alone our children's children. Talk with your children and love them. Try to help them scripturally, not through threats and legal tactics. An ill rebuke stirs up strife. All children are not the same and some things will not work with others. But in all cases, love for the parents and love for the children is the true answer. Love does not allow a parent to come between their children and grandchildren, it will cause people to work through compassion to see a family made whole and work as a unit. Any other tactic is not from God and should be dealt with as a manipulation ploy of the enemy! You ask, what about the negligent parent? The LORD says when thy father and mother forsake you, I the Lord will lift you up! What more assurance do we need? We have a Father that sees and knows all! We seem to have problems believing that at times. Remember, children are a gift from God! These children belonged to Him first!

Brothers and sisters should respect their own, however Cain and Able show us this problem existed from the beginning of time. One was jealous of the other. One wanted to be recognized because he gave from what was left rather than what was first. This is so as we live on the earth. Family members devise plans to uproot other family members. Family members stand as wedges between other family member's children, causing a curse to be upon those children, and resulting in covetousness of the other family member's family, something God speaks expressly against! Can two wrongs ever equal a right? Not as I was taught. You see, it all surrounds the idea of inheritance! You can only receive an inheritance through relationship. If your relationship with the parents is good, so is your inheritance. If it is bad, so may be your inheritance. It is really common-sense relationship math but, the devil convinces you it should be all or nothing no matter the cost. On earth the benefits may be sweet but in eternity they will probably not be so sweet. As we live on earth, so shall we be known in heaven. How are you known, not by your friends but by your family? Are you being a loving person, standing for right or are you being divisive and manipulating in your family dealings trying to keep others from the blessings of the Heavenly Father and of their earthly father? I could chase a few rabbits down the road on convenient sacrifice of time and money but would rather not but feel it is worth mentioning anyhow.

This coming year, I would implore each person to pray for reconciliation of families! If you are not doing your part, I will be praying for you to have your part truly revealed to you and that you will have the trust to follow Christ into that part. If you have been divisive, I pray that you will repent from that mindset and become a person with the mind of Christ to become a person of reconciliation. If you are a manipulator, I pray that God will help you to get away from that form of witchcraft and you will no longer be a witch trying to control all things around you. If you are harboring resentment, I pray that God will allow you to be set free from that vice and make amends with those that are close to you. If you are a gossiper, I pray that your speech will become wholesome and speak on those things that are good. I pray for family relationships to be restored throughout the world that man can see God in a new way and the "sons of God will be manifested," as the world groans to see these things.

I realize this is a tough message, but we must begin with ourselves! I pray that God will bless those this year that have been living through these things. May God give you all wisdom, strength and power to make the right decisions in tough times as you move forth during this year! May you all pray for us this year as we seek the LORD in these very matters. If you are not the victim of these things, you may be the perpetrator. One place or another, we may have work to do, should you be involved in these situations. God Loves the Family Unit! It was designed to have dominion over all things except each other. May we see this original design restored as we go through the next year! May families learn to live together in love for one another.

7 - An Everlasting Fellowship!

David Makes a Covenant with Jonathan - 1 Samuel 20

Jonathan knew David was going to be made the King of Israel. He knew how the order of things went as this happened. He knew his family would be endangered and exterminated. He had such a relationship with the King-to-be, he approached him and made an agreement with him. The Lord tells us we can boldly approach His Throne of Grace. We can confidently ask God for His protection over our family. We find a type and shadow of God's commitment to us in the reading below:

1 Samuel 20: *14 And thou shalt not only while yet I live shew me the kindness of the Lord, that I die not"*

This is not about Jonathan's life only! This is about the kindness he is negotiating for in regard to his offspring. This is what Jesus does for us. When the Hebrews left from Egypt, they were told to put lamb's blood over the door post and they and their family will be saved. In Acts 10, the house of Cornelius, Peter told Cornelius, you and your household will be saved. Apply the lamb's blood over the door post of your family entrance and watch what God will do.

1 Samuel 20; 15 But also thou shalt not cut off thy kindness from my house for ever: No, not when the Lord hath cut off the enemies of David, everyone from the face of the earth. 16 So Jonathan made a covenant with the house of David, saying, Let the Lord even require it at the hand of David's enemies."

So, a negotiated agreement was reached, and a covenant established.

David Takes Over as King - 2 Samuel 2

After the death of Saul, David became the King of Israel.

Existence of Jonathan's Son Revealed - 2 Samuel 4

2 Samuel 4; 4. And Jonathan, Saul's son, had a son that was lame of his feet. He was five years old when the tidings came of Saul and Jonathan out of Jezreel, and his nurse took him up, and fled: and it came to pass, as she made haste to flee, that he fell, and became lame. And his name was Mephibosheth. (1 Chronicles 8: 34 And the son of Jonathan was Meribbaal; and Meribbaal begat Micah.)

The revelation of Mephibosheth's condition as a result of a fall signifies the crippled state to which we are born. The name Mephibosheth actually means "Idol Breaker." The number five actually symbolizes Grace throughout the Bible. Grace will indeed describe the life of Mephibosheth as the "Prevenient Grace" was arranged by his father.

David Unifies a Divided Israel - 2 Samuel 5

David's first priority as King was to unite Israel.

David is Reminded of His Covenant with Jonathan - 2 Samuel 9

2 Samuel 9: *1And David said, Is there yet any that is left of the house of Saul, that I may shew him kindness for Jonathan's sake?*

Time has come to honor his covenant with Jonathan! The fullness of time has come for restoration.

2 Samuel 9: *2 And there was of the house of Saul a servant whose name was Ziba. And when they had called him unto David, the king said unto him, Art thou Ziba? And he said, Thy servant is he. 3 And the king said, Is there not yet any of the house of Saul, that I may shew the kindness of God unto him? And Ziba said unto the king, Jonathan hath yet a son, which is lame on his feet."*

Ziba knew about Mephibosheth and his general whereabouts, perhaps because he would have been his servant since he was Saul's servant.

2 Samuel 9: *⁴ And the king said unto him, Where is he? And Ziba said unto the king, Behold, he is in the house of Machir, the son of Ammiel, in Lodebar."*

Lodebar means without pasture or Desert area. This is in an area believed to have been on the west side of the Jordan River in the Desert's edge.

2 Samuel 9: *⁵ Then king David sent, and fetched him out of the house of Machir, the son of Ammiel, from Lodebar."*

David put out a search warrant for Mephibosheth to bring him to the King. Now, let's fast forward a little bit to the Book of 2 Samuel and see where things are coming together. We see a little of what jealousy can do when someone gets an idea of taking what is rightly yours.

Mephibosheth's Little Talk with the King - 2 Samuel 19

2 Samuel 19: *24 And Mephibosheth the son of Saul came down to meet the king, and had neither dressed his feet, nor trimmed his beard, nor washed his clothes, from the day the king departed until the day he came again in peace."*

Mephibosheth had low regard for the king and himself at first record.

2 Samuel 19: *25 And it came to pass, when he was come to Jerusalem to meet the king, that the king said unto him, Wherefore wentest not thou with me, Mephibosheth?"*

Why didn't you follow me back? Mephibosheth begins to tell the King how he was conned. The world had fed him a bill of goods.

2 Samuel 19: *26 And he answered, My lord, O king, my servant deceived me: for thy servant said, I will saddle me an ass, that I may ride thereon, and go to the king, because thy servant is lame. 27 And he hath slandered thy servant unto my lord the king; but my lord the king is as an angel of God: do therefore what is good in thine eyes.*

Mephibosheth recognizes the King for what he is. He recognizes his position, authority, and standing with God.

The Con Game - 2 Samuel 16

2 Samuel 16: *1 And when David was a little past the top of the hill, behold, Ziba the servant of Mephibosheth met him, with a couple of asses saddled, and upon them two hundred loaves of bread, and a hundred bunches of raisins, and an hundred of summer fruits, and a bottle of wine. 2 And the king said unto Ziba, What meanest thou by these? And Ziba said, The asses be for the king's household to ride on; and the bread and summer fruit for the young men to eat; and the wine, that such as be faint in the wilderness may drink.*

A word picture of the last week of the life of Christ and establishing the New Covenant.)(Remember, Jesus rode in on a donkey, shared a meal and later broke bread and drank of wine with the disciples in the upper room instituting what we call the "Lord's Supper."

2 Samuel 16 *3 And the king said, And where is thy master's son? And Ziba said unto the king, Behold, he abideth at Jerusalem: for he said, Today, shall the house of Israel restore me the kingdom of my father.*

Today is the day unto salvation: Today is the day of restoration!

2 Samuel 16 *4 Then said the king to Ziba, Behold, thine are all that pertained unto Mephibosheth. And Ziba said, I humbly beseech thee that I may find grace in thy sight, my lord, O king."*

Ziba was operating with jealousy in wanting the very things Mephibosheth was going to receive. Deception at its finest. There are groups of people who will throw you under a bus to get what you have. It is all works of the flesh.

Mephibosheth continues.

2 Samuel 16 *28 For all of my father's house were but dead men before my lord the king: yet didst thou set thy servant among them that did eat at* *thine own table. What right therefore have I yet to cry any more unto the king?*

All my family was dead, and you set the servant at the table. You gave him what belonged to me, so to speak. You have allowed the servant to eat from your table or commune with you. I have no room to say a thing. (Aren't you glad Jesus made it possible for us to live again with God through Him?) Judas betrayed Jesus at the Last Supper and Jesus' own said not a word.

2 Samuel 16 *29 And the king said unto him, Why speakest thou any more of thy matters? I have said, Thou and Ziba divide the land.*

Pretty much the King had decided and that was all there was to talk about.

2 Samuel 16 *30 And Mephibosheth said unto the king, Yea, let him take all, forasmuch as my lord the king is come again in peace unto his own house.*

Mephibosheth didn't want compromise, he wanted to go all in. It was all or nothing for him! That is how we must be; ALL or Nothing! Jesus doesn't want part of us, He wants All of us.

Mephibosheth before the King - 2 Samuel 9

God is the God of second chances, and third, fourth and so on.

2 Samuel 9 *6 Now when Mephibosheth, the son of Jonathan, the son of Saul, was come unto David, he fell on his face, and did reverence. And David said, Mephibosheth. And he answered, Behold thy servant!*

Mephibosheth arrived, humbled and repentant, willing to serve the king.

2 Samuel 9 *7 And David said unto him, Fear not: for I will surely shew thee kindness for Jonathan thy father's sake, and will restore thee all the land of Saul thy father; and thou shalt eat bread at my table continually.*

I had a covenant with your father and will honor that covenant. I will take care of you as I promised, is what David was saying.

2 Samuel 9 *8 And he bowed himself, and said, "What is thy servant, that thou shouldest look upon such a dead dog as I am?"*

When a Kingdom changed hands, the entire linage of the previous king was wiped out so there was no legitimate heir to the throne. It doesn't matter your current situation, God has a Covenant, and it includes you! You are not what you may think, you are precious to God!

2 Samuel 9 *9 Then the king called to Ziba, Saul's servant, and said unto him, I have given unto thy master's son all that pertained to Saul and to all his house.*

Restoration is taking place right here. That which was taken is being restored. Those things the enemy has taken from you will be restored. If you want some things back you once cherished and the enemy took, seek God and watch Him work. Not saying you will get them, but you may gain peace over not having them. God is a God of Restore!

2 Samuel 9 *10 Thou therefore, and thy sons, and thy servants, shall till the land for him, and thou shalt bring in the fruits, that thy master's son may have food to eat: but Mephibosheth thy master's son shall eat bread always at my table. Now Ziba had fifteen sons and twenty servants.*

Elevation to your rightful status will be given to you. It is a time where God will make you stand out amongst those who thought differently of you. A time to shine bright in the world of darkness! He will have people working for you that thought they could maintain a stronghold over you. God is a God of Reversal!

2 Samuel 9 *11 Then said Ziba unto the king, According to all that my lord the king hath commanded his servant, so shall thy servant do. As for Mephibosheth, said the king, he shall eat at my table, as one of the king's sons.*

Joint Heirs with Jesus God will send in workers to help where you can't seem to get things done. God is the God of Gifting and Provision!

2 Samuel 9 *12 And Mephibosheth had a young son, whose name was Micha. And all that dwelt in the house of Ziba were servants unto Mephibosheth.*

God is a God of Family! Micha was right there with Mephibosheth, his father.

2 Samuel 9 *13 So Mephibosheth dwelt in Jerusalem: for he did eat continually at the king's table; and was lame on both his feet.*

We can be restored spiritually and may still be physically disadvantaged.)

God is a God of Everlasting! Like Mephibosheth, we can all eat at the King's table, continuously!

Fulfillment of Covenant - 2 Samuel 21

2 Samuel 21 *7 But the king spared Mephibosheth, the son of Jonathan the son of Saul, because of the LORD's oath that was between them, between David and Jonathan the son of Saul.*

The Lord will spare those who he has sought out, have humbled themselves, changed their ways and committed to serve Him, with all they have as the reward for His New Covenant and your new life.

Mephibosheth's life was one of anything but comfort and convenience. He was discomforted by the fall. He was uprooted and moved to a place of lack at the tender age of five. His family was gone. He was orphaned and living in a foster home. He had physical issues with his feet that restricted his walking and working. He had people trying to take what was rightfully his. BUT God! The grace of God flowed into his life through the King David. It matters not your condition, your past or your present, the King of kings and Lord of lords has sent out a search party for you. He wants you to return and dine at his table and have your needs supplied. God wants to Bless you today! God has sent out a search warrant for you! He is the Judge, the Holy Spirit is the Sheriff, and Jesus is our Defender! It is easier to surrender than to run.

The Lord himself gave an ordinance to the church, His redeemed people, as a way to remember His sacrifice on Calvary for us. As we prepare for the Lord's Supper, please take a moment and check your heart? Come to Him with a clear conscience. Let all the old garbage go. If you don't know Jesus as your personal Savior, now is a good time to make that decision. Please join with us as we celebrate what Jesus has done for us?

1 Corinthians 11:23-26

8 - It Is Well! - Genesis 50

There is a young man in the Bible who is resented by his brothers because he was shown favor by his father when he received a coat of many colors. He received a special covering from the father and his brothers were enraged. They threw him in a pit because he had seen things and received things they were not privileged to receive. This young man was sold into slavery by his own brothers, worked as a slave in Egypt, was accused of sexual immorality, imprisoned but yet, found favor in God's eyes.

Years had gone by, famine had hit the land, and this young man had risen to such a stature in Egypt that he oversaw all the provisions of the people.

The brothers who were in need, had to approach him and ask for help. Let's pick up in the Book of Genesis and Chapter 50, beginning at verse 16:

Genesis 50   *16 And they sent a messenger unto Joseph, saying, Thy father did command before he died, saying,*

The Father gave instruction to forgive and the specifics in the next verse. God always teaches us what to do in situations so we can move past them.

Genesis 50 *17 So shall ye say unto Joseph, Forgive, I pray thee now, the trespass of thy brethren, and their sin; for they did unto thee evil: and now, we pray thee, forgive the trespass of the servants of the God of thy father. And Joseph wept when they spake unto him.*

At the words of the messenger, Joseph's love for his brothers was revealed through compassion, as he wept.

Genesis 50 *18 And his brethren also went and fell down before his face; and they said, Behold, we be thy servants.*

His brothers were honoring the instructions of their father, albeit they were hungry and in need, like the Prodigal Son in Luke, they were ready to submit and be his servants. Perhaps you may know someone who is hungry and in need. In need of the feeding of the Word of God, His Grace and Mercy. Someone who is willing to submit life in the service of God.

Genesis 50 *19 And Joseph said unto them, Fear not: for am I in the place of God?*

Joseph was quick to let his brothers know, he is not God and he is not to be feared. He is pointing out that the issues are between them and God and not them and Joseph.

(Account of the Merchandiser who helped us in Concord, NC)

Genesis 50 [20] *But as for you, ye thought evil against me; but God meant it unto good, to bring to pass, as it is this day, to save much people alive.*

Joseph did not exactly let them off! He called them out. He let them know, their plans were thought as evil, intended to harm him. BUT GOD: used all the things he went through, all the things others and his brothers put him through as a path to accomplish that which was good for the people. The plan to saves lives of many. It was a time of refining. Time spent in the Refiner's Fire. Not all things we go through are attacks from the enemy. Many times, our trials are misunderstood and are really a God process for our growth into purpose.

Joseph had been through some stuff! Often, we feel we have been in that pit, with nobody to help us out!

We often feel we have been sold out and feel we are caught up (wrapped up) in bondage!

We are often falsely accused!

BUT GOD:

We serve a God who:

- Turns Coal into Diamonds!

- Sand into Pearls!

- Worms into Butterflies!

- God can turn your life around!

Today, I speak these words of life to you. The time of pressure, the time of grinding, and the time of containment is over!

Step into your new identity! Your identity in Christ!

Become that precious jewel!

Fly in this world that was created for you!

Genesis 50   *²¹ Now therefore fear ye not: I will nourish you, and your little ones. And he comforted them, and spake kindly unto them.*

God will nourish you and your family! There is absolutely nothing to fear!

Isaiah 26   *²⁴ Trust ye in the LORD for ever: for in the LORD JEHOVAH is everlasting strength:*

God is your everlasting strength! He has a purpose for your pain, a reason for your struggle, and a reward for your faithfulness! Trust Him and NEVER give Up or Give In!

And in a time when things were not looking good for his country, Zechariah had this to say in:

Zechariah 1:13

Zechariah 1 *¹³ And the Lord answered the angel that talked with me with good words and comfortable words.*

All is good today! Rest in the Lord! Things around you may look bad but, as a Child of the Only True and Living God,

All is Well!

Invitation:

We all go through times where we are tested and refined. Today is the day to declare completion and move into the New Year with a fresh start in service of the Lord! A time of Thanksgiving! A time of fruitfulness! If that is you this morning, reach out to God! He is waiting! God is faithful!

9 - *Ministry, Near and Far*

Introduction: Welcome everybody to the 132d Anniversary Celebration of Mount Olive Baptist Church! As we, at Mount Olive, reflect on what the past year has included and how God chose to use us, we stand amazed at what the Lord has done. If you would, turn in your Bibles with me to Acts 1:8. Mount Olive Baptist Church loves God and God loves them.

Acts 1:8; *"But you shall receive power, when the Holy Spirit has come on you, and you shall be witnesses to ME in Jerusalem, and in all Judea and Samaria, and to the ends of the earth." NKJV*

The Saints of God at Mount Olive have received the power of the Holy Spirit as He has moved on them. They have evangelized in their Jerusalem, the city they love, Bonifay, Florida.

Mount Olive strives to fulfill the duties of the church:

1) Waging War through Spiritual Warfare and the powerful weapon of Prayer

2) Continues to Run the Race and persevere in the work of Christ

3) Serves the Mount Olive Community through and in the Love of Christ.

Mount Olive is not only a church in name but is the Church in Deeds inspired and led by the Holy Spirit!

Mount Olive reaches into the community through the Women's Missionary Union (WMU) by:

1) Sponsoring a local elementary classroom. Not only in school supplies but in other areas of need.

2) Establishing a scholarship fund for High School Seniors through an Essay competition and process of judging.

3) Providing handmade baby quilts to the Pregnancy Center at HCBA.

4) Reaching out to families as an expression of love at special times of the year.

As a church, Mount Olive has presented ministry opportunities to Holmes and surrounding counties through the ministries of:

1) Mutzie — Christian Comedian and Compassion Ministries Artist

2) Carroll and Donna Roberson

3) Squire Parsons

4) The Chronicle Gospel Group

5) The Wilson's (Who are with us again today)

6) Four Plus One from FBC Bonifay.

Mount Olive is a faithful contributor to the Holmes County Baptist Association (HCBA) through the Cooperative Program, giving 10% of income monthly.

Mount Olive has been faithful in supporting:

1) Florida Baptist Convention

2) McQuire State Missions

3) Florida Children's Home

Mount Olive has supported the recovery efforts in Livingston, LA in a cooperative effort with HCBA, West Pitman Baptist Church and pastor Eddie Eaton, reaching out to a church that was flooded. The Deacon of Glory Baptist Church, Deacon XXXXX, and his wife, XXXXX are with us today and we are proud to call them good personal friends and to Mount Olive Baptist Church.

Mount Olive reaches into the Yucatan Peninsula in the little town of Progresso. For the last 2 years, we have supported efforts to get school supplies to an orphanage in Merida through a local man named XXXX XXXX. We also contribute to the Assisted Living home in Progresso. We do street ministry as an expression of love for the day we are there. The average daily wage in that area of the Yucatan is $1.00 a day. We do this on the annual minister's cruise out of Mobile or New Orleans.

Mount Olive contributes to the SBC's Cooperative Program and supports the Lottie Moon and Annie Armstrong Missions offerings which support national and international missions.

Mount Olive is striving to become the triumphant church God wants her to be! We are busy at Mount Olive! We know we are only scratching the surface of what needs to be done. We are striving to do more! We are praying for church growth! This church of 34 members is busy doing the Lord's work and making changes for the Kingdom of God.

You have heard some of the things God has had the Mount Olive congregation doing outside the doors of the church building. Every person in this church body has a place to serve. We all do something and that something makes the whole body more effective. God intends for His Saints to serve, and that we do.

We are not a perfect church because we are all people. We don't always agree on everything, but we agree to not be disagreeable. God is plain in Psalm 133: "Behold how good and pleasant it is for Brethren to dwell together in Unity…" We understand: All we do is worship and service to God and unity brings the blessings of God on the work He leads us to do.

We gather every Sunday morning at 9:45 AM for Sunday School and 11 AM for Worship Service. We return on Sunday nights at 6 PM for Bible Study. On Wednesday night at 6:30 PM, we meet for corporate prayer. It is during that time that we pray for each of you. We pray for every church, every pastor and leader, and our missionaries and teachers. We pray especially for the law enforcement community that keeps us safe and the first responders who come to our rescue. We do not only petition God for others, but we also give God Praise for what He has done, first and foremost. We enter His presence with Thanksgiving in our hearts and give Him praise. We utilize what E. M. Bounds referred to as the most effective weapon in seeking to help others, the weapon of prayer.

When the congregation has nothing else to do, and is not together in these forms of ministry, they are about the community serving through individual ministries:

1) Hospice volunteer

2) Family Crisis and Pregnancy Center Volunteers

3) Many in less visible areas of service

4) Providing Christmas gifts for families (Children)

5) Providing food to those in special need

6) Oftentimes providing financial assistance to others

The Saints at Mount Olive are always busy about the Lord's business. Some more visible than others but, all of them are at work!

In case all I have mentioned is not enough, there is building maintenance, cleaning, yard and garden work and seemingly ongoing projects of update and repair. There has been so much work done in and around the church and the cemetery, I can't even remember what timeframe it has been done in. We have just completed the renovation of the kitchen area in the Fellowship Hall, which you all are invited to see as you join us for a great meal after service.

All of this takes valuable time from each person. Brother XXXX from the West Florida Baptist Association told me not to long ago, for a small church (and he reminded me, we are small) Mount Olive is certainly a busy church!

My wife, Cheryl and I are honored and proud to be a part of Mount Olive! I am more Humbled to be called their "pastor." I love these people and I love you all!

We can do these things, only because God sent Jesus to be born of a virgin named Mary, lived and ministered until He was hanged on that old, rugged cross. But that is not the end! God is not dead! Jesus rose again on the third day and ascended into heaven and sits on the right hand of the Father. He left us to be His body and His presence on earth. We should exemplify Jesus, as the role model and become His presence in the community and world. It is to God's Glory we do these things! It is about you that we serve the Lord! It is about you that Mount Olive exists today at 132 years of age! It is you that is our focus in love and about the Heavenly Father in our service. Jesus paid the price to make all this possible!

To God be the Glory!

10 - My Greatest Calling

(My Parents' Need was my Greatest Call)

As almost all children do, they reach a point in their life that they leave their parents' home and begin life for themselves. I was no different! Though I was out of the house, living my own life, my parents were still concerned about my well-being. They prayed for me, called me, helped me in time of need and above all, they loved me! They loved me unconditionally! They loved me in the years I wasn't living right and through the years of rebellion and irresponsible behavior. They loved me through my years or alcohol abuse. They loved me when I didn't even love myself. They gave selflessly in an effort to guide me to a better path.

It was not their fault I was where I was. All my decisions had me where I was. I was where I was because God had called me, and I was in rebellion towards Him as well. I had a higher calling but wouldn't accept it.

In 1998, I finally stepped into the ministry with my wife Cheryl and our daughter Jessica. We went through some fast-paced training by the Holy Spirit and into the pastoral ministry. From pastoral Ministry, the Lord sent us to the mission field to become church starters in central Texas. After a couple of years on the US mission field, we returned close to home to pastor a church and ultimately start another. We were back close to home and our parents.

Years had passed and my parents and I had worked to restore the relationship with them that I had seemed bent on destroying in my earlier years. One day in 1993, the Lord had spoken clearly to me that I should find something my Dad loved to do and take him to do it. I quickly reminded the Lord that nothing was my fault between my Dad and me. How wrong I really was! At any rate, the next thing the Lord spoke to me was so real, it shook me. The Lord told me that I needed to be friends with my Dad regardless of whose fault I felt it was because he would not be around much longer.

As we all know, our definition of time doesn't always equate to the Lord's meaning of the same statement. So, I called my Dad and asked him about going to a NASCAR race with me at Daytona in July. He said, "No." I thought, "So there God, I tried!" God would not allow that to be the final word. I knew Dad liked going to Atlanta, as did Mom. We got some tickets for the Atlanta race and invited Dad again. This time he said, "Yes." We had a good time. His comment to me on the way out of the track area was that he couldn't wait to get back next year! I was glad we had finally started to build a relationship that I had hindered all these years.

The following year, we got Dad into the Pit area and in the garage to meet the drivers and crew chiefs and owners of the cars. He was able to see many of his old heroes of racing!

We were in Joe Nemecheck's hospitality tent where Dad had the chance to really spend some time with Joe and his wife Andrea. Dad was thrilled.

We took Dad to the Indianapolis Motor Speedway and to Talladega. Dad and I had a good time. All this was done before we took our first step into the ministry.

What I know now is, it was essential this relationship between my Dad and I be repaired and restored prior to me going into the ministry or the ministry God called us to would not blossom.

We stayed in daily contact with my folks while we were out of the area. God had been good to us and sent us back home to be around them in 2002. This was 9 years after the restoration of our relationship began.

Mom and Dad celebrated their 50th wedding anniversary in June 2003. The Family gathered at Mary Mahoney's Restaurant in Biloxi for the celebration. As God would have it, there was a Newlywed couple celebrating their wedding at the same time that day and Mom and Dad were able to be an inspiration to them as they had begun their journey in life together. In the early months of 2004, Dad and Mom had been to visit Virginia and spend some time with my older brother Ray and his family. When they returned home, Mom became rather ill. She went to the hospital and they admitted her for bronchitis. As the tests were conducted on her, things began to not look so favorable for her. They diagnosed her with pulmonary fibrosis, a lung condition that causes the lungs to become hard and no longer flexible not allowing oxygen to enter the blood stream. It is a disease that is extremely cruel in the way it does your body. It affects the body chemistry of blood gases to get out of whack. The Drs also detected an arrhythmia problem with her heart during that time and performed a procedure to correct that problem.

Several days later, they wanted to release Mom from the hospital, but she told them she was weak and dizzy and her vision was blurry. What was not being caught was the massive internal bleeding she was suffering because of complications from the heart procedure. Mom had just had her first of several brushes with death that worked on her over the next 3 years. She was placed in ICU immediately, given many units of blood, and placed on non-invasive life support. With some words of knowledge from the Holy Spirit, a doctor that would listen, and a nurse that made the call, checks on Mom's condition began and the problem was isolated by the doctors as spoken by the Lord.

I sat in the hospital cafeteria that day and talked with my Dad. His life was shattered. He told me that it wasn't supposed to be that way. He said he had always planned that he would go first, and he was struggling with the issues at hand. I could do nothing but listen. What could I say to a man that was first, my father, and two, been married to the same person 50 years! I had no idea the pain he was going through or what he would endure over the next 6 years.

Mom spent the next 6 months in hospitals and nursing homes along the coast. She was in and out of Intensive Care Units with blood infections and other respiratory issues and near death a couple of times.

We stayed with Mom one day when they were moving her back to the nursing home from the hospital because Dad was in Jackson working with a church ministry. As they were moving her back to the nursing home, the ambulance turned on their lights and took off as fast as they could safely go. Cheryl and I knew this was not a good thing. They got Mom to the nursing home and placed her on 125 percent oxygen. The nurses said they were prepared to place a resuscitation tube down her if she stopped breathing. This was something Mom had said expressly that she did not want. Dad came in and we spoke to him about Mom's condition. They met with all the nursing folks and Mom signed a living will and power of attorney saying she did not want to be resuscitated should she stop breathing.

Cheryl and I had stayed the night with Mom and had Dad go home to get some rest. The Lord had sent me to Mom's room at 430 in the morning, from the waiting room, to pray for her healing. Dad and I spent the morning in the cafeteria as I listened to him trying to sort out what was happening with Mom. While Dad and I were downstairs, the Dr was upstairs taking the oxygen mask off Mom and turning her oxygen down to 1.5 liters. That was a far cry from the two hoses they had hooked to her mask cranked wide open. Finally, Dad and Mom were getting some relief. Mom ended up moving back to Ocean Springs to the Nursing Home to be closer to home. She was given one bunch of bad news after another. She was told she would never walk again and be confined to a wheelchair because of the leg she had broken during all the different transitions. To Mom's delight, she had some praying Nurses Aides that visited her daily. We would visit with them and Mom too and we watched as God answered and began to transform and heal her. Dad was spending as much time as he could with her. By Thanksgiving, she was up walking with the help of a walker and cane. Mom was home for Christmas after a 6-month battle and over 2 million dollars in medical expenses.

Mom was doing well and Dad was doing better with the issues facing them both. Mom was out and about without a cane and walking well in pretty short order. She went to see the orthopedic doctor who told her she was a walking miracle and had a miracle to be able to walk. We were comfortable she had won her fight! At least for now!

Our youngest daughter had graduated from High School and we had the opportunity to work on the road. We hit the road, trying to get home as much as possible. We would work the west coast for three weeks and fly into Dallas, TX, drive to Mississippi and see Mom and Dad then fly to the East coast for 3 weeks. We saw Mom and Dad every three weeks. They would never complain and if asked how they were would always say they were doing ok. When they were asked if they needed help, they would refuse, not wanting to interfere with our life.

We were home-based in Texas and were pastoring a church in the small town of Breckenridge, Texas. Because of the massive travel starting to take its toll on us, we sought employment in Texas and found it. We had been working on a Wednesday and got home after service on that Wednesday night had ended. I was in the sanctuary picking on my guitar and talking to the Lord. The Lord spoke to me and told me, the day is coming you will have to place your family before the church and the church will understand. I had no idea what that meant at that moment in time. It was about two weeks later when I found out. I had called Dad and spoken with him. He seemed distant and I wasn't sure what was going on. He had been having some issues with diabetic ulcers on his legs and had his legs wrapped. I wasn't sure what was going on, but I knew it wasn't normal for him. It wasn't but a few minutes later, Mom called me back and told me that Dad was having trouble. She said all he would say is that he wanted to go home. He didn't know where he was. I told her to call the ambulance and get him to the hospital now. Her problem was the house was locked and she could not get out of bed either because of her issues progressing and causing her to become weak. I contacted my sister and brother at that point and asked my sister to hurry and get to them since she only lived 50 miles away. When the paramedics arrived at the house, Dad's blood sugar had dropped to 23. He spent the next week in the hospital. We already had our marching orders from God to help them! Place them first in all things.

Mom's health was going really fast when we returned home. She was in her last days. Dad was trying to recover from his own health issues and needed rest. Mom ended up in the hospital the last of November 2007 in Intensive Care. Dad stayed with her during the day, and we stayed with her at night. Mom called me to her bedside one night and told me the Lord had just spoken to her and told her that He was going to see her through this, and she would go home. She was happy to know she was going home but the home God was speaking to her about was not the one she was thinking about. We watched Mom fade away, day by day, getting weaker all the time. On the morning of December 7, 2007, Mom was called to eternal glory by the Lord. Dad was both shattered and relieved, if that could make sense to most people. He was relieved Mom was not having to suffer anymore but shattered because a big part of him was now gone.

We had moved home to help Mom and Dad and we struggled with the failure to be able to do anything to help Mom in this case. I asked God many times, why could we pray for so many people and see them healed and receive a miracle but yet could not get a breakthrough for my Mother. On the way home from the hospital Dad told me not to take what he said wrong, but he said he was glad that this was over. He was tired and he was tired of seeing Mom suffer so much. He had been dealing with these issues with the heart of love he had for Mom and wouldn't ask for any help until it came to a point where he just couldn't do what needed to be done by alone. Dad had truly demonstrated what Jesus said about no greater love has a man than he will give up his life for another. That is where Dad stood on Mom's health issue but when it was all said and done, he had done all he could, and Mom still passed away. Dad asked me on the way from the hospital to please don't run off and leave him. Now the real point of why God wanted Dad's and my relationship restored. Dad would need us in the end and we too would need him.

I will never forget, as we were going back to Texas to get our belongings, I was speaking to God about whether I was doing the right thing or not when He told me, Randy, I have never told you to honor your father and mother that I didn't know these days would come. He assured me that He would take care of us. That He has done!

After Mom passed away, Dad and I had a lot of time to spend together. Dad traveled with us in the ministry and become known by all our friends in the ministry simply as Dad. He was blessed to meet people like Ira and Judy Milligan who took time and interest in the ministry at the hospital Dad was doing as a volunteer. He met many others but these two were his favorite people. Dad had the chance to hear me minister and see God work through us on many occasions but after about a year, Dad started to want to slow down from the ministry. He traveled with me to Bloomington, IN, a town he wanted out of as soon as he got there. He did not like that place but enjoyed the travel. By the end of the year 2009, Dad had started talking about death more and more. I would just make a comment of encouragement to him and go on. I have learned that I should have probably talked with him more about it as opposed to discounting his concerns and perhaps fears.

In mid January 2010, the Lord woke me up in the middle of the night and spoke the words that Dad would not be with us by June because he would pass of renal failure. It came with such peace, but it sure hit me hard. What do you do with something like this? I tried to be more attentive to what Dad was saying and watching him ever so closely.

One morning in March 2010, around 330 AM, I walked into the living room and Dad was sitting up in his recliner with the lights on. He was more relaxed than I had seen him in a long time. I asked him what he was doing up so early. He told me that he would tell me because I would believe him and not think he was crazy. He proceeded to tell me that Mom, Pastor Rutrough, Pastor Hansen and Pastor Hansen's wife had all been in the living room visiting with him for about an hour and a half. All four of these folks were and are passed on to glorious eternity. They were all really close friends on earth. Dad said he told them he wanted to go with them as they were leaving. They told him that he couldn't go yet but they would be back to get him. Dad knew his days were short on earth and so did we. We continued to watch Dad have issues with his body shutting down. He couldn't shake a cold any longer and he couldn't seem to stay out of wound care with leg issues.

By the time our youngest daughter was graduating from college, Dad was so weak he didn't want to attend the graduation in Mobile. That was the 8th of May 2010.

I arrived home from work on the 12th of May and Dad had told me he went to Cardiac Rehab and they told him he had congestive heart failure, go to the emergency room and check in now. Dad came home instead. I asked him if he wanted me to take him to the emergency room and he said no. Dad went to his bedroom that night to sleep, something he hadn't done since Mom passed away. At 3:30 AM on the 13th, he yelled for me to get him out of bed. Dad was beginning to have more troubles of his own. He thought he had misplaced his billfold and I was in his car looking for it when he realized it was still in his pocket which had flipped up and was above the belt line of his pants. I was beginning to see something was drastically wrong with dad right then. He told me at 4:30AM he was ready to go to the emergency room. We got into the car and I drove him there. By that time, he needed help to get out of the car.

The ER doctor said he had bronchitis and may have the option of going home to get well. I knew this wouldn't be an effective way to recovery for him based on what had been happening in the past few months. I also knew the two encounters from Dad and I since January. I told the doctor that he should not give Dad that option.

I went to work and checked on Dad that day on several occasions and had pastor Bolden checking on him since they too were really close. Dad seemed to be doing pretty well with the antibiotics they gave him. Things were looking good. I was thinking that this was one time I had missed God on hearing His voice and I was glad! Dad felt pretty good!

The next morning Dad called me, and all his hope seemed to be shattered. The doctors told him he had congestive heart failure, COPD and renal failure. He had pneumonia and it was very aggressive. Dad asked me to bring him some clothes for his Hospital Auxiliary Executive Board meeting for that Monday.

I brought him clothes and he attended his meeting. He was in two hospital gowns, in a wheelchair with oxygen during the meeting. He told the board they should take a real close look at him and see his example that this is what 5 years as the auxiliary president would do to a man. He had a conversation with the board and told them he was a dying man and that they needed to push on without him.

Right after the board meeting, I was supposed to be able to pick Dad up and bring him home. When he returned to his room, his blood gasses were so off that he had no idea who he was, where he was or where he lived. The nurses called me and told me that he was in distress. By the time I got to the hospital, Dad was letting the nurses know what they could and couldn't do to him. When I walked in the room, Dad knew immediately who I was and began talking with me about his condition. The Drs decided to keep him a few more days to get him situation under control.

That afternoon, Dad told me he wanted me to stay with him because he knew that I understood. I am still not sure what I was supposed to understand but I did understand the major calling in my life to honor my parents!

I stayed with Dad from that point except for the night of the 21st of May. I watched Dad suffer from much of what Mom suffered with in her years of dealing with COPD. Dad didn't know anyone in the room with the exception of me. Dad was fading and fading fast. Dad and I experienced the trials of pneumonia as the temperature swings would have him freezing the burning up. He was getting so weak that he couldn't stand up, but he still tried, and I helped. He was not well. On the 20th of May, Dad was growling like a bear in the early morning. Not being a stranger to people in the active stages of passing, I knew this was what is referred to as a "death rattle." We spoke to the Dr and asked him what was actually going on and if there were any options available. Dad had said absolutely no life support measures. He believed if he did not have quality of life, his purpose was fulfilled.

The Dr gave us one option with a proviso time limit. The issue was Dad was incoherent and non-responsive to the medical staff. I told the Dr I would ask him and if he agreed, we would do that but if he doesn't respond, he has already said what he wanted and that would not change. I spoke to Dad and he answered me. I asked him again and asked him if he knew who I was. He answered me by name and told me to tell them to hurry. As they rolled Dad to ICU, I told him that I love him. He told me that he loved me too and never forget that! I knew these might very well be the last words Dad spoke to me.

In the middle of the night, Dad's kidneys quit functioning altogether. There were no further medical procedures that could be done that would not be invasive and be very painful, neither of which Dad wanted. Dad was taken of the machine and placed back on the ward.

At the early hour of 155 AM, I saw two Angels appear in dad's room as God seemed to open the curtain to the spiritual for us to see. I woke Cheryl up and had her stand on the right side of Dad and I returned to his left side. I began to thank Dad again for everything he had done and how I appreciated and loved him for being the Dad he had been. Dad loved to hear me preach so I began to remind Dad about the scripture in Genesis 5 about Enoch walking with God. I explained that where the first time the word "walked" is used, in the literal Hebrew language it means "chased after" So this being the case, it means Enoch had a point in his life that he began to chase after God. There is a verse that speaks to the number of years that Enoch chased God, representing one's lifetime. The next verse says that Enoch walked with God and he was no more. In that usage of the word "walked" it literally translates to "caught God" or "caught up with" God. I told Dad that he was just like Enoch. He had been chasing God for a long time. God was now right in front of him, and he should grab God's coat and go home with him, that we would be ok. Dad, who hadn't moved in nearly 24 hours, turned his head to the right to acknowledge Cheryl and then turned his head to the left to acknowledge me. He then turned his head straight ahead, took 2 more breaths and passed. We watched the light literally leave the mortal body as Dad went home with God.

Dad is no longer in the physical but is eternally with the Father in heaven now! It doesn't make life any easier for us without him, but life has to go on regardless. Dad was not only my Dad as he passed but he was my best friend, next to my wife. I can only say that because of what God had told me to do some 16 years earlier.

Yes, I have a call to minister to God's people across the globe, as He leads. My first calling is to my family. I have learned that my calling starts and finishes at home. I have learned that in this calling for the family, I should take more time to listen to my family members about their issues. Above all, I have learned the importance of relationship with our parents. God doesn't care about who was right or wrong, He just wants someone to be willing to stand up and make the first move of reconciliation. God has charged us to take care of family members, especially our parents. As for me, there has been no higher calling that gave such satisfaction as serving my parents in their last days!

This calling and assignment didn't end with my parents passing. As with all people, when life here is over, there is unfinished business to attend to. My parents were strong Christian people that had lived a long life based on integrity. They handled all their business well and kept their word to people and met all obligations. Dad had named me as the Executer of his estate matters since Mom had already passed and Cheryl and I were with him. Since Dad was very private about his business dealings, we elected to allow things to sit for about 6 months to see what may filter in before opening the estate and perhaps finding things that surfaced after the settlement. This would add to the expenses that would be incurred settling the estate, should issues like that arise. We retained an attorney and began the process of estate settlement. There were some issues that could have been left alone, such as the home mortgage, once the estate was signed off on by the judge. That mortgage could legally stay in Dad's name and we just needed to continue on paying the monthly note, as we had since Dad's passing. Because of the way Dad and Mom lived their life, we wanted to clear their name and let their good names rest in peace with them. It took a little more time and effort to refinance the home and get all things with our parent's names closed out. Our desire and thinking were to close the chapter on their life as a completed story, without blemish, just as they had strived to live.

It would be so easy for us, as people, busy in our own desires, to turn a blind eye and deaf ear to the needs of those that sacrificed and raised us. The neglect towards parents and parent abuse is one of the most serious things going on around us today. Elder abuse is more common than child abuse. It is so easy to get caught up in other things and develop an attitude of "ingratitude" towards our parents because we lose sight of the price, they paid to get us where we are. We get caught up in retirement, retirement funds, big houses, nice cars and big boats so much that we don't have time for the ones who spent time with us. The Evangelist that was preaching the night I came to the LORD, Sammy Hall, did then and still does sing a song by Cat Stevens in every ministry opportunity he has. The song is titled, Cats in the Cradle." It is a story of a parent that was to busy for the child and when the child grew up and the parent wanted to spend time with them, the child didn't have time for the parent. Many times, our parents work long hours to provide for the family. We get bitter because we didn't have time spent with them when we wanted it. Then when the parents get older and are in need, the children reciprocate by shunning the parents. We are in such a sad state of affairs with how we are treating our elderly today. We want to shove them into nursing homes and assisted living homes just so they don't interrupt our plans in life. We justify it by rationalizing, they didn't spend time with us when we were young so who cares? This is what God was preparing me to get beyond when He told me to make amends and be friends with my Dad.

The world tells us to seek those things we want in life and go after them, forsaking all others to get there. The world tells us happiness is measured through bank balances and prestigious jobs. The world tells us success is predicated by the possession of worldly goods. I have come to understand that success is doing the will of the Father, both natural and Spiritual without compromise and complaint.

There is Biblical order and there are Christians that can tell you all about what the Bible says but will not put their faith in God for His promises in these issues. Many say that the scripture says to count the cost, but may I say, the costs have already been paid by Jesus! It was only me that I was concerned with about walking in disobedience in the issues of tending to my parents, not my older brother or younger sister. It was about my relationship with my parents and the willingness to sacrifice the little we had to care for and love them. They were worthy of the same sacrifices we made for the Lord when He sent us to the mission field to start churches.

Though Cheryl and I have worked in many facets of the ministry by being church planters, pastoral couple and evangelist and view them all to be a great calling from Christ, my greatest calling was serving my parents in their time of need!

God Bless You All!

11 - Order of Service for a Believer's Funeral

Making An Everlasting Mark

- **Procession**

- **Prelude** (Music Playing)

- **Invocation:** Beloved, let us seek comfort in the assurances of the Word of God: Our Heavenly Father, the source of all comfort, our Peace in the hour of dying, we thank thee for your Son, Jesus Christ, who through grace and power gives us life and immortality beyond this present moment. We seek Thy comfort in this time of sorrow. We seek Thy strength trust to undergird our frailty. May the blessing of Thy peace be our eternal hope, through Christ Jesus our Lord, Amen.

- **Congregational Hymn:** "When We All Get To Heaven"

- **Obituary/Acknowledgements**

- **Special Music:** "Winner Either Way"

- **Eulogy** - **Making An Everlasting Mark:**
  Joshua 4:1-8; When all the nation had finished passing over the Jordan, the Lord said to Joshua, (2) Take twelve men from the people, from each tribe a man. (3) and command them saying, "Take twelve stones from here out of the midst of the Jordan, from the very place where the priest's feet stood firmly, and bring them over with you and lay them down in the place where you lodge tonight. (4) The Joshua call the twelve men from the people of Israel, whom he had appointed, a man from each tribe. (5) And Joshua said to them, "Pass on before the Ark of the Lord your God into the midst of the Jordan, and take up each of you a stone upon his shoulder, according to the number of the tribes of Israel, (6) that this may be a sign among you. When your children ask in times to come, "What do those stones mean to you?" (7) Then you shall tell them that the waters of the Jordan were cut off before the Ark of the Lord. When it passed over the Jordan, the waters of the Jordan were cut off. So these stones shall be to the people of Israel a memorial forever. (8) And the people of Israel did just as Joshua commanded and took up twelve stones out of the midst of the Jordan, according to the number of the tribes of the people of Israel,

just as the LORD told Joshua. And they carried them over with them to the place where they lodged and laid them down there.

- Vs 6 asks, "What do these stones me to you?"

- To answer this question, let's look at the stones that are placed on the monument and memorial Brother Paul Strickland placed for the world to see:

- First and foremost, the most important stone and the foundation is the stone of **Family**. We need only look within the people around us today to see the love of his life for (#) years. And never did a conversation with him go to completion until he spoke of one of their offspring. Brother (name) loved to see that polished stone that was rounded out with the wives of their sons who he never called daughter-in-laws, he emphatically called them daughters. Then there are the hosts of grandchildren he loves and cherishes.

- The second stone on the monument is the stone of **Country/State/Community**. As one of the first two people chosen to enter a new field of club management for the US Air Force, he was a trendsetter in his field. The family traveled with him to some places across the globe while waiting patiently for him to return home from other places they could not go. Brother (name) worked to educate the youth in the dangers of street and illegal drugs through the D.A.R.E. program and Law Enforcement. He would be out there directing traffic in the worst of weather to keep families and children safe. He once shared with me about the scant amount of room he had when directing traffic at the school.

- The third stone is the stone of **Service to God**. He became committed to service to God upon his conversion experience and grew in Grace as he learned. Much like Jesus who is said to have grown in both wisdom and stature. Brother (name) grew into different places of service to the church but more to the service of God. His growth led him into being a Deacon, Trustee, Treasurer, and his mastery of stewardship of the affairs of God. His life models integrity and is a faithful witness to what God did in his life and will do in yours. Even into last weekend, he was witnessing and praying for the medical staff that dropped by to visit with him.

- The collection of stones is his legacy! Those stones are cemented together by his relationship with God. His love and confidence are demonstrated by his ability to look adversity in the face, stare it down and WIN proved it! We have bug people come by the house and help us to get rid of bugs: we call those people Exterminators. We have Arnold Schwarzenegger in the movies, and he is called the "Terminator." In knowing Brother (name) and his resolve to the work and will of God, I would call him "*The Determinator.*" He wanted God's will to be done!

- Brother (name), MS (name) and I went to visit Brother (name) and MS (name) one Thursday evening. Brother (name) was doing what he loved to do. He was carving on this walking stick. He showed me the stick and the carved faces on the stick. What I noticed was, the faces all seemed to look like him. I asked him: "Brother (name), how come all these faces look like you?" He held the stick, beside his face like this and said: "Selfies!"

- I dropped in on him before taking off on vacation and as I was leaving, I told him: "Brother (name), don't be running off before I get back." In his quit wit he said, "If I do, I'll see you on the other side."

- Brother (name) loves people and did everything with consideration towards others. His biggest desire is to see each one of you, his children, grandchildren, family, friends and neighbors, to have the benefit he spoke to me in saying, "I'll see you on the other side."

- So, in closing, the question to each and every one of you is: "What do those stones mean to you?"

- **Prayer:** O Thou the God of all comfort and compassion, look upon these the bereaved, whose hearts are heavy with grief. Let now the ties that have been broken be bound by Thy love and their faith in Thee. Through this experience, grant them the strength to offer themselves in dedication and service to Thee, it is now in the name of the Lord Jesus Christ our Lord we submit our petition, Amen.

- **Recessional:** The services here are now concluded; let us proceed across the street where Interment will take place.

- **Reading during Recessional:**

- **Committal:** (Done Graveside)

- **Closing Prayer:**

12 - Paul's Thorn in the Flesh

2 Peter 3:16 makes it clear that even Peter had some trouble deciphering the writings of Paul. Peter says they are not easily understood by those that are unlearned and so it is with them with the other scriptures as well allowing them to believe things of their own thoughts, which are not correct. Now that is Randy's take on what that particular verse is speaking to. But one such example of what Peter was referring to is found in 2 Cor 12. Here Paul has asked the Lord to remove a thorn in the flesh he had, and he has pleaded with the Lord three times about it. Christ finally responds by saying, "My grace is sufficient for you, for in weakness I am made perfect."

Some believe this scripture points to a physical ailment that Paul had, and others have even speculated that perhaps it was a wife or ex-wife. Some use this scripture to justify their own physical condition saying, "God would not heal Paul; therefore, I am going to be like Paul and remain sick, calling it my thorn in the flesh."

That viewpoint may be a justification for one's physical condition in their own mind, but it is the easy way out and lets God off the hook for not healing them. Jesus went to the whipping post and took a severe beating to bring healing to all people. In fact, He did that on His way to the cross signifying that healing came before salvation. Oftentimes that is the case. That is why Spiritual gifts are important and alive in the church today, regardless of what others may say and what you might believe. People who receive healing should be a walking testimony to the gifts that God has placed in the world through His people. The only problem is, we don't want to endure the persecution that comes from being that witness. We don't want to get into the Book of Acts and really become friends of God as the name Theopolis really signifies. We like the scripture where Jesus tells us to pick up our cross and follow Him, but we don't want to be crucified on it for Him.

Paul had the Damascus road experience of conversion where he was struck blind. Ananias was sent to pray for him, and the scales were removed from his eyes and he was able to see. God did not partially heal Paul's vision. God healed Paul's vision. So that kind of knocks the vision thing out of the picture for us. There is also talk of other issues that I have yet to find scriptural documentation to support. One such scripture that cannot be supported, unrelated to Paul is the shadow of Peter passing over people and they were healed. That scripture says people laid their sick in the street so that if Peter's shadow was to pass over them, they might be healed. No clear support of the actual happenings. Let's look at the reality of what people are trying to do here. They are simply looking for an excuse for their condition. Paul speaks to the things he was subjected to as he was serving God. He says he took 40 lashes minus 1, 5 times, he was beaten on his feet with rods three times, shipwrecked three times, and once even bitten by a viper which didn't harm him. He was locked in prison after prison. He was stoned and left for dead, with other Apostles watching, and yet, he got up and walked into town the next morning. All of the abuse that were placed on him was meant to kill or cripple him. Paul was able to continue walking after his feet were beaten. He was able to take a continued stand for the Lord after receiving 39 lashes, not once but 5 times. He was stoned and could talk about it and was healthy! Because of Paul's numerous healings, I am convinced that the issue Paul is speaking of is NOT a physical condition.

The scripture says that because of the great revelation Paul received, there was a messenger from Satan sent to buffet him. This messenger was sent to keep Paul from getting too big headed! It was there to keep Paul balanced. He speaks of being in heaven. When Jesse Duplantis spoke of being taken to heaven, Hank Hannagraff was quick to post that Jesse was a false prophet. The reason Hank did such a thing is because Hank personally has not had that experience and believes because Hank hasn't had it, nobody can! Paul battled with the same issues. Others couldn't get a hold of what Paul was talking about! They would get mad at him and do things to him to get him to quiet down. The thing is none of it worked.

Can we see that the thorn in the flesh was for Paul's own good? Can we realize that what was going on with Paul also happened to Joseph in the book of Genesis when he revealed his dream to his brothers! Didn't Joseph endure persecution but was actually right in what he said? King Solomon asked God for Wisdom and that wisdom was to care for God's people. We need to use wisdom in dealing with people in the church. Paul needed to use wisdom in dealing with the people of his time too. He also said he had the weight of the churches on him! Man, do you realize that churches beat pastors and try to cripple them? Do you know they even try to kill them by destroying the message and mission they have been given? You show me a pastor or minister that has been through these things and I will show you a pastor that can relate to Paul and probably has some real power in their ministry! You show me someone that has endured these things and I will show you a balanced minister!

We all like to have these preachers visit that look like the seminarian we find in the Book of Acts; a man name Apollos. He was educated in the school of schools back then and he was a good orator. He was a convincing speaker and used the scriptures to prove Christ! He knew only about the Baptism of John or about salvation. He had no real power in his ministry!

He was taken in tow by Aquila and Priscilla who showed him the way of the Lord more perfectly. He was educated by people that didn't have the word taught to them but had experienced the "WORD" in their lives. There was so much missing from what Apollos was doing that when Paul came to Ephesus the first question he asked was, "have you received the Holy Spirit." If you have a minister that cannot provide for the growth of the people, he is of no use to the people until he receives the Holy Spirit.

The only problem with Paul was, he knew too much. He had seen heaven and was excited and wanted to tell the world, but the Lord didn't want that done. Not because He doesn't want you to know, you simply can't handle but so much of these things at a time! Jesus said it this way, don't cast your pearls to the swine! Don't tell too much too soon to people who cannot accept it! Paul was stopped by the Lord from telling too much by a tactic from God to allow a messenger from Satan to push against him no matter where he went. It happens to us too! God can use the devil too! There have been times in all of our lives when we were discussing things and were on the verge of telling something when a phone rang or somebody else walked up and interrupted and we didn't tell it! We are quick to blame that stuff on the devil but why can't we simply praise God and thank him for keeping our mouth shut, even if He chose the devil to do it?

Paul endured much for the sake of the Gospel message. The church loves to quote the scripture "if a person comes to you and brings a gospel to you other than the one we have brought to you, then you should put them out." The truth be known is, if you were to hear the gospel that Paul taught, you wouldn't recognize it! Paul taught the cross of Christ in all walks of the life of the believer. His epistles talk about the person's life and the cross, a person's ministry and the cross, the church and the cross and the list goes on. It is about "cross-style living." The gospel Jesus taught is foreign to most today! We seem to be caught up on the gospel of salvation when Jesus came and did so much more!

One of our church members had an issue we were unaware of. The Lord showed it to me as I was standing over him in a dental chair pulling concertina wire from his teeth with a pair of pliers. I got to the last blade and it wouldn't come out of his teeth. The Lord told me to cut it off as it was that man's thorn in the flesh. We went to his house and spoke with him. I told him what the Lord had shown me. I had no idea what was happening. The man began to tell me that he knew what the vision was about and that he couldn't quit speaking evil against his stepfather. I told him I had no idea of what he was talking about. He proceeded to tell me that he couldn't stop speaking ill of his stepfather. He said stepfather had shot and killed his mother in the kitchen of their home in the presence of the children! I told the man that God said it was alright, He understood, and that His grace is enough.

Healing is a divine thing, no matter how it comes! We watched the demonstration of the healing of a man with a brain aneurism while we were in Texas. He had twenty-three immediate family members that were all Jehovah Witnesses. The Lord spoke to me the things that would transpire. I called the man's daughter-in-law and relayed the information to her. As it happened, the Lord did exactly as he had said he would do! By Friday of that week, the nurses told the man there was nothing wrong with him and to go home. The doctors refused to see him anymore. Why was this important? Some little Baptist church in Dallas, TX gained twenty-three converts that Sunday morning! All to the glory of God!

It brought balance and understanding to a family because of the trials of another family member that held strong to the word of God and was healed!

We are no different than Paul and must guard ourselves. It is easy to get arrogant as God uses us. We must have a way to attain the balance needed to be effective in the ministry. Sometimes God provides the balance through adversity that we would rather God take away than for God to allow it to work in us. Without it, we would not be balanced and would be ineffective!

Therefore, the revelation that I have received on this scripture is far from the traditional lack of healing issues that unlearned ministers try to purport it to be. They simply don't understand what Paul was writing and turn it to mean something that it really doesn't mean at all. Some would even argue that I could be wrong in the revelation that I have received on the scripture and its subject matter, but I would say to you, Prove it! I have presented enough to you this morning to prove it was not a physical condition, now, what else can it be other than a spiritual condition?

As we seek healing from God, we may have issues we have to get through to get a physical healing but first and foremost, we must seek God for the spiritual healing that brings forth the physical healing! We have to realize that the word of God is clear in that is says what a man believeth in his heart, so is he! If you want to believe something contrary to what Jesus and the word of God says, that is your right, but it is only you that is being cheated! You should start your physical healing through the spiritual healing that must precede it! If there is something in the spiritual that is hindering you, God will speak the same words to you he spoke to Paul, "My grace is sufficient for you...." You will then be healed. It is simply between you and the Lord. Paul was only expressing some issues he was going through! He was not trying to tell anyone that God was not going to heal him.

13 - Selecting Leaders - Acts 6

Acts 6:3-4; *"Wherefore, brethren, look ye out among you seven men of honest report, full of the Holy Ghost and wisdom, whom we may appoint over this business. But we will give ourselves continually to prayer, and to the ministry of the word."*

One of the things that we have seen in church planting is placing leaders within the church too early. There are some key things that the Lord speaks to us about in this area. He instructs us to know those that labor among us. We should be fully aware of people's character before placing them in office. If people are different in church than they are at work and at home, chances are the true person will come out and it will not be good for the work of the ministry. I know many church leaders that you can walk up on at work and you would be surprised to find out they went to church at all. Beware of these people. They are still in the flesh and can only see and do business in the flesh. The only people that can be consistent in their behavior are those that are sold out to God. Yes, they will have times that emotions will run away from them and they will say things that they shouldn't but, that doesn't mean they are not good for the church.

Finding biblically qualified leaders is a time-consuming process. Paul wrote to young Timothy and told him to lay hands on no man suddenly. There are some strong payments that will be required because of this. Just because someone has been in church for thirty years is not a reason to make that person a leader. I know of people that have been to church for 50 years and finally accepted Christ as their personal Savior and they have served in leadership positions for most of those 50 years. How many ministries do you think these people affected and how much of it was adverse or could have been? Do you think they were ever instrumental in destroying an individuals' life in the ministry? What would your responsibility be for disobeying the Word of God? A church will affect the lives of countless people during its existence, and we should do all things with due diligence in selecting proper leaders. The church's effect should always be positive. These people will likely be there when you leave, and they will be a direct reflection on you and your leadership.

When the first Deacons were placed into the church, there were thousands of people within the church. They were elected to be table waiters. They were to be servants and no more. They were to serve the people at the direction of the pastor. They were an extension of the pastor's ministry that would prove to be indispensable later. These folks have a position that is not one to be envied in the church today. They catch all the flack and must be ready to take a stand on the word of God and work with the pastor at all times. They are not however intended to be spiritual leaders in a church. I am not trying to be hard on Deacons! I am pointing out that their responsibility has been turned into a form of authority over the years through controlling and manipulation tactics that have caused many a minister trouble. The first Deacons were selected because they were born again believers; filled with the Holy Ghost, full of wisdom and of good report (Acts 6:3-4). They were capable of preaching God's word and serving people. Serving the widows was their primary function. Many times, a person wants to become a Deacon because of power and control. It will become his church! We must be careful who we place in positions that the line of good stewardship is not crossed to personal ownership. Deacons have been allowed to gather so much power and control that the churches are being sold out to personal agenda. The life expectancy of a church is no more than 50 years with a wavering trend after the first ten years resembling a roller coaster. A lot of this is because we are not cautious about who gets placed as leaders within the new works.

Although the Bible only addresses Deacons and Ministerial positions in placement, I believe we must watch the other leaders we place as well. It is the duty of the church planter to guide and direct, but the planter must also maintain control without being controlling. We would be wise to not have leaders in a church before placing someone that is not spiritually ready into a position.

As we look into selecting our leaders, there will be people that show up and are eager to serve. Many of them may come to you with a history of serving other churches. Learn what you can about them from talking to them. Be sure you check to see that they are doctrinally in line with the work the Lord has sent you to do. God speaks of a group of people called the Nicolaitanes whose deeds He hates (Revelation 2:6). These are people that have gone from church to church, not able to get a strong enough following to start their own work but are strong enough to do some really bad damage to the mission God has you on. They are direct messengers of Satan coming to destroy what God is doing. They are people on assignment. They look and talk like Christians, but they are surrounded by their own selfish ambitions to do things their way. They have God all figured out. Beware of anyone that thinks they have God figured out!

We have had people come into a new work and they seemed dedicated until you watch their tithing habits and their commitment to the work. If people are coming into the church and tithing to outside ministries as a main source of tithing, they are not supporting the work that is going on. These people are merely making a show. We had a man in a church that tithed two dollars in seven months and then wanted to run the church. Make sure you look for the fruit of spiritual maturity as you move forward (Galatians 5:22-24). These people will not be doing things the way God has instructed us to do. Their rebellious actions to God's Word will reveal them...

1Timothy 3; and Titus 1 instruct us on the way we should elect leaders of the church. I would like to say first that these are two pastoral Epistles that are designed to educating pastors in selecting leaders. The pastoral Epistles, though educational for all, deal directly with the selection of the church leaders. It is not healthy for churches to call pastors based on worldly belief and with the carnality that exists in most churches. Many churches cannot properly discern what God's will is for them. God said that people would hold to the traditions of men as opposed to the commandments of God. The traditions and teachings of men will make the word of God of no effect. This is taking place every day in the church. There are cries there are not enough pastors willing to fill pulpits. There is just not enough money to pay our pastor! May I be so bold as to say, most of these problems are self-inflicted. These churches have become a revolving door ministry for many pastors. The churches expect more from pastors than they are willing to give. They want the pastor and His family to make big sacrifice and be the only ones to walk by faith. This evolves from the teachings that we choose who we want and decide who are the called messengers of God based on do they match up to what we think and what the denomination says. Though denominations serve a good purpose, God cares less about denomination than the human soul. The churches of today should carefully and objectively look at calling a pastor and see what the Lord requires of them as well. This is an area that should be taught as the church is founded (1 Corinthians 9).

The denominational talk is that Paul was a tent maker. He was a bi-vocational minister. Paul didn't get money from the churches! Paul, although he was a tent maker, he was not a pastor. He was an Apostle by his own admission. He was sent by God to start new works all over the place. If we look into 1 Corinthians chapter 9:7-14, we will see that Paul is writing to the church in Corinth and explaining what their duties are in providing for the pastor. He did not take anything, lest they suffer but once a pastor was there, it was their duty to support him. We also find this in the book of Exodus as we see the tribe of Levi being formed and the duties of the tribe outlined. We can even read further into the Word and find that once the tithe from all the tribes was taken to the Tabernacle, 10 percent of the tithe was offered up to God and the Levites got the other 90 percent. Now if that won't rock the foundational ground of the commitment for what churches believe in pastoral support, I don't know what can! Perhaps, the old argument, we just don't have enough rings a bell for some of us. The Book of Acts says that people sold their homes to give the money for the continuation of ministry. The intention of the scripture is to do what it takes to hear and carry the message of God no matter what you may have to give up. I would not suggest you beat up on people about selling their homes to do something for the church. God will have them do that, if need be. All I am saying is, when you leave the church plant, do your best to have people ready to provide for the pastor and support them fulltime.

I am not ashamed to admit that we have some things we call distinctives within denominations. We were in church the other day and an Evangelist began to talk about how he was told by God to baptize his brother. This was significant as the man's brother was suffering with terminal cancer at the time. The man had accepted Christ and requested to be baptized. One of the old Doctrinal positions is Baptism by immersion. While I believe it is Biblical to baptize this way, I do believe God honors our obedience to the act of baptism. The Evangelist was told to use a bowl full of water and sprinkle the water on his brother's head. I asked him how that changed his theology about baptism. The Evangelist was not ordained or licensed either. (I'm sure that it doesn't make his brother any less baptized.) The response from the evangelist was simply "Exactly!"

These two scriptures outline the life and conduct of people in the desire to be in the office of Bishop and Deacon. I can assure you one thing; I had no desire to be a pastor, but God had a plan! There are many people who live a good life and can meet these qualifications. There are a lot of good people in the church. There are those that have much wealth that people like to get in position as an avenue to more money. There is so much that can be read into these scriptures about qualifications. It is the only area that describes the conduct of the Deacon's wife. In fact, the wording for the wife of the Deacon would take you straight back to the word "Diablo" which in Greek means Devil or Satan when it refers to the slanderous gossip that the wife must refrain from (1 Timothy 3:11).

There are issues of divorce that come from these scriptures. It would be better to see a divorced, born again believer serving in any of these offices as opposed to those meeting worldly qualifications and have never come to experience Jesus as their Savior. At least the born-again believer is forgiven by God. Who really cares what man has to say? God says the reason we are not to select, and He is talking to pastors here, is that:

"For there are many unruly and vain talkers and deceivers, specially them of the circumcision:" Titus 1:10 (KJV)

He is referring to those caught up in religiosity or legalism in this verse.

God is not saying that these people shouldn't serve on account of their past experiences but because of the present performance of the religious legalists in the church. I am not sure that I can go along with the scriptures being interpreted as they are sometime interpreted. There are some that take this as a solid rule that women cannot serve in pastoral roles and there are those that believe this issue is addressing the area of divorce. Through study, I am convinced that regardless of what we think, we must know that God calls pastors and people to serve. We can either seek His wisdom in all matters or become pious and cold about them. A word of caution would be to check every situation and ask the Lord about it. Once the church begins to seek God, He will begin to do His work through them. If we are to take the critical text approach to interpreting the scriptures in these two letters, we can go back to the issues of polygamy being addressed. With the way we watched the fall of King Solomon and King David before him over the wife situation, it would be very practical for God to say one wife is fine because I created you to have one but no more. Women were never allowed to have more than one husband so there would never be a reason to address the marriage issue to them. Had God not intended for women to be used in pastoral roles, He would have never sent Paul to help Lydia and we would still be hearing Paul's words of shout trying to figure out what God was doing to him (Acts 16:6-15).

God is no respecter of person and to give a person that has been divorced and remarried a different set of rules makes Him respect someone that hasn't had problems in a different light. God says there is neither male nor female in Christ (Galatians 3:26-29). I believe God can use who He wants, when and where He wants to accomplish what He wants. We simply must be willing, as church planters to pray over all these issues. They are sure to come up as you go along. We will eventually learn that we can be conservative and even fundamental in our beliefs, but the liberality of the Love of God will begin to become evident in our lives. This doesn't make you a liberal or any leader you select a liberal either. This kind of love enables your leaders and others, as well as you to see people purely as the Lord sees them through Jesus.

It would be better for the sake of the Lord's work to have a person that is poor and hard working but loves God and meets the qualifications in Acts 6 to be a Deacon or church leader than it would for someone to meet the qualifications in 1 Timothy 3 or Titus 1 and does not have a relationship with God. A personal relationship with God, through Christ is essential in selecting your leaders. Hey, if you can find a rich person and they meet all the criteria listed in every place, get them! Don't sell God's church out by placing worldly leaders in charge.

14 - The Cross Makes Us Vulnerable

I had a revelation on the crucifixion of Christ as it pertains to the church and covering the other morning as I drove to work. I will attempt to expound on this as I seek to hear God on the revelation.

Christ on the cross as man, embracing man yet becoming all sin. Arms outstretched to receive man into him (as God) yet man though lifting him up, killed him by piercing his side with a spear, where the rib was taken from to form woman (church/Body of Christ). Again, His arms were the covering for the church (Body) but yet man went under the covering to expose the weakness and strike the body causing His death.

This is a revelation of what Paul writes about in Ephesians where he says that Christ gave His life for the church. The paradox is this, Jesus gave his life for the church but yet the church became His life existence and continuance on earth until His return. This expresses the magnitude of the love of God for mankind expressed through His only Son. Then, because we do not have the presence of Christ in His fullness, we now have the Holy Spirit to minister to us, speak to us, teach us and lead us in our service as part of the Body of Christ. When the Holy Spirit becomes our leading, He becomes our mind, we receive the mind of Christ and we can become one with and in Him. This is the oneness Jesus prayed for us in the Garden in John 17.

When Jesus spoke to His disciple, John, from the cross, He transferred the care of the woman, His mother, to John or mankind. Here we see the picture of the transformation of the church from a single body to the single body, yet all inclusive of those who will come into the body. Man was charged with making that happen by Christ from the cross.

The revelation of the birth and creation of the church and its vulnerabilities at the cross of crucifixion become more evident the more I seek the meaning of the cross. The church was in conflict from the beginning. It was at odds with mankind. It was under terrible scrutiny throughout the ministry of Christ, but it was centered then simply on Christ. The major turning point of the church, where it become a world-wide body came at the cross, followed by a short 50-day period, called the Pentecost, where the church pulled into itself, the body functioned as one, and then the mind of Christ came to them in the power and demonstration of the Holy Spirit, bringing forth the convergence of the Kingdom of God into the world in an instant! What was used to denote the most horrible form of death to the world became the sweetest and most treasured birthplace of what is now known as the Body of Christ! Genesis 50:20 says what man intends for evil, the Lord will use for Good, is definitely the case here too.

The power of the cross is incomprehensible to me at this point. It is much more than a place of crucifixion of one Messiah with two gangster men in a single day. It is more than the place of sins being taken on by the Savior sent to redeem us. It is more than the physical torture Christ endured. It has a very deep spiritual meaning to us all. It begs the question, why do we think and believe the church should not be persecuted in modern times when it was birthed in persecution through the very Body that brought it? Why should we believe it should be a place protected from attacks of the enemy or mankind in the flesh when the cross and the crucifixion present that very picture and message? The crucifixion became a necessary means to have the presence of God, through the Body of Christ present in the entire world once again. Until Christ came, we never heard about God's presence anywhere but where His chosen Hebrew people were as He was confined to the Holy of Holies in the Temple. He resided with His people. Christ's whole life was for the ministry of reconciliation of the Kingdom of God with the entire world. His Body has to encompass the world to make that happen. In order for that to transform, He had to give up His earthly body for the spiritual being He was in the beginning. This freed His presence to all! This is the significance of the veil in the temple being torn from the top to the bottom. It was God above, ripping the veil to allow His presence to come out! His grace poured upon the whole world, not to a select group of people any longer. It was as if God reached from His throne and grabbed the top of the veil, much like we would do a sheet of paper, or the NYC phonebook, and ripped it in half while it hung in His hands. When we tear something in half, we are in the act of destroying the original product or altering it for a different purpose, because it is no longer needed for its original purpose. This is the same with the veil. With Christ's work on the cross, the veil was no longer needed, and God tore it in half. The veil was destroyed, and God's presence was opened to the world and its people immediately!

It was through the vulnerability of the physical body of Christ that we have been graced with the faith and drawing to become one in Him with God. It is with this same vulnerability that Christ suffered through the church should be willing to suffer through in opening up the way for all mankind to enter into Him.

A reflection of the crosses on the hills as they relate today may be something like this. We have the Red Cross, the Green Cross and the Blue Cross in our modern nature of speech. I don't know of any others that are really well known across the globe but these three, in particular have universal recognition in the world today. Looking at them one at a time, the Red

Cross is the symbol of immediate help or First Aid. When a crisis comes into an area of our life, help comes in the way of "First Aid." Sometimes it is a cut or injury and other times it is a national disaster through some form of devastation. But we all understand the "Red Cross" and its use.

The "Green Cross", though not as well known as the other two represents "Safety". If a person is seeking a place of safety writings and crosses will be in Green to signify that. This place of safety is a refuge during a time where hurt or pain may be evident to the extent of personal injury or life.

Things that provide safety are things like ear plugs, safety glasses, steel toed shoes and the like. We place these things on to guard from injury. We also retreat to places like shelters to find safety in bigger storms.

The "Blue Cross" represents a place of health care or restoration in our physical bodies today. Hospitals and care clinics are the places mostly associated with the "Blue Cross".

So, if we placed these three crosses before us today for the world to see, what would we see? Are we as a Body of Christ, providing the "First Aid" furnished through the "Red Cross" by reaching out to help others in their times of real need? I emphasize real in need because sometimes a person's need is not a need but rather a want. I have refused to give people money who were asking, saying they need it for food, while yet they have a pack of cigarettes in their pocket. They should re-evaluate priorities in their money spending and make a sacrifice, not infringe on your goods to support habits that are not beneficial for them. But a person in need requires attention and they need it right then. They don't need political baggage and procedures to stand in the way but need help finding the way.

These people, the church should reach out to render that "First Aid" to. We should become the good Samaritan even if it means opening ourselves up to criticism from the mainstream of Christianity that is refusing to help. We must be that "Red Cross" first aid station for the wounded. We must be willing to help in tough times. We do that for our own family! We call ourselves a church family but yet we are oftentimes quick to deny our own Brother or Sister, of help.

The "Green Cross" represents a place of "Safety". As a church, we must become that place of safety where people feel they can come, in their troubles and be safe. Be safe from attacks from the outside? Yes, and from the inside as well! There are people reluctant to provide this safety because it may present a bad image to the local population. What concern should we have of that? Jesus wasn't concerned about His image on the cross, He was concerned about your soul and your destiny. He was concerned about your relationship being restored with the Father through what was happening with Him. He gave up

His physical body to become a Spiritual Body encompassing all believers as one. He endured the present persecution for the greater end.

We, as a part of the Body of Christ should be willing to stand strong and take that persecution why knowing the greater end by providing safety to people. Why did I choose to place the "Green Cross" in the middle? Because Christ was in the middle and He is our place of safety!

The "Blue Cross" is the third cross we know off and will look at. The Blue Cross signifies a place of restoration! It is a place where a person has time to get medical attention for what ails them. It is a place where people are made whole and can go back to living a normal life in many cases. As a church body, we should be aware that some people come to the church like a hospital. They only come when they need attention and healing. They are only there to get through a tough hurt or pain. Once through that, they oftentimes leave.

Many times, all three crosses are at work in the lives of people coming into the church doors. But here we are seeing the restoration of people. Many people have spiritual hurts and pains. They have been through shunnings, so called church discipline, church conflicts and other issues involving churches because of various beliefs. They come to another hospital looking for a place to be healed and get along with what happens or is to happen in their life. We should be that hospital, regardless of what their hurts may be. Like many people who go to hospitals get healed, leave and never return. That is ok with the hospital and it should be ok with the local assembly, knowing their purpose for that person is complete. People should come and go in the local assembly; we shouldn't be the cause though. We, as a local assembly, should provide what is required for a person's restoration to wholeness, regardless. There is nothing more important than a person's eternal salvation and redemption.

So, as Christ's death on the Cross provides us wholeness, so should the church be emblematical of the same. We should be the first place a person can run for and receive help! We should be the First place a person can and will run to for safety! An above all, when people arrive, we should be the very place people can be made well. Not all people who come in needing First Aid will live in Christ, nor will they stay in a place of safety or remain at the hospital or place of restoration. If we do our ministry well, we will have return people who are willing to help and bring others in needing help and sharing the same desire of help. It is unrealistic to think we can retain everybody, even some that have been around for years we just perform our purposeful work in the body. If not, we have simply become another building with a few people going through some motions of idle works affecting nothing!

It took it all! It took Jesus coming down from His Throne in Glory to the earth as a baby. He endured this life to prove it is possible to fulfill the law through Him, but in Him, we don't have that concern. He died on that rugged Cross to bring forth His body to us to come into. He was vulnerable and did not run! He was all powerful but yet never shunned His assignment! He died a physical death but rose again to guarantee what He said will be carried out! He sits on the right-hand side of the Our Father in Heaven, mediating for us. We are in Him as one! He sent His mind in the form of the Holy Spirit to guide, teach, heal and lead us in our purpose in this life. And last but not least, He has not forgotten us, and He will finish the entire act of redemption one day!

Are we ready as a Body to allow man to persecute us while we embrace mankind as Jesus does and leave our very weakest point exposed to the enemy even unto death for the mankind we are embracing? My prayer is, Lord, let my legacy reach beyond where I stand and be as far reaching as you will take it in helping others to come into your Body.

Scriptures used: Luke 23, Matt 27 & 28, Isaiah 9, Isaiah 53, Acts 1 & 2, John 17, John 19, Genesis 50, Luke 2, 1 Thessalonians 4, Hebrews 9, Genesis 2, Ephesians 5

15 - The Sick Shall Be Healed

Mark 10:15-20; 15 And he said unto them, Go ye into all the world, and preach the gospel to every creature. 16 He that believeth and is baptized shall be saved; but he that believeth not shall be damned. 17 And these signs shall follow them that believe; In my name shall they cast out devils; they shall speak with new tongues; 18 They shall take up serpents; and if they drink any deadly thing, it shall not hurt them; they shall lay hands on the sick, and they shall recover. 19 So then after the Lord had spoken unto them, he was received up into heaven, and sat on the right hand of God. 20 And they went forth, and preached every where, the Lord working with them, and confirming the word with signs following. Amen.

The Lord Jesus gave us specific instructions to go into the world and carry the gospel to every creature. I would like to address this in the context of divine healing as well as the scripture reference to healing above.

We had a Pomeranian named Cowboy. He was my wife's dog. He had little to do with me unless there was something wrong with him. If he were feeling a little under the weather, he would climb up in my lap and lay there. He wanted me to pray for him. If he didn't get in my lap, he would come and put his head under my hand and just stand there. I would pray for God to heal him and he would return to normal. Cowboy got hit by a car and died. The veterinarian said that judging by his teeth and health, he looked to be about 2 and a half years old. Cowboy was pretty well preserved by the Lord as he was 8 years old. God had taken good care of him and divine healing had helped to keep him that way.

In verse 17, we begin to see the things that Jesus says believers will do. He is so specific that He says that we will lay hands on the sick and they shall recover, if we only believe. Jesus never said that we would lay hands on the sick and they may recover sometime or whenever He feels like letting it happen. He says straight up, it will happen! Verse 20 says that the believers went everywhere, the Lord working with them, confirming His word with signs.

This is an awesome thought and feeling. I taught divine healing for a long time believing that God healed. We saw and experienced many people being healed and miracles happening all around us. It was definitely a time that signs and wonders were following because God was working with us and He was confirming His word. It was then that the LORD placed a minister by the name of Maurice Sklar in our lives at the Skillet's Restaurant in Brownwood, Tx. We had seen much happen in a ministry trip to

Mexico and had just returned in February 2002. As we ate, we began to speak. It was then that not only did I believe in the things I had been teaching but God began to confirm them in my own life. It was in that small restaurant that we were with 3 other ministers that I received 4 miracle healings within a matter of minutes. The word of knowledge came forth and Maurice had revealed my health issues one at a time and them ministered healing to me. I had my back straightened, my hearing restored in my right ear, where everything was garbled, a detached retina repaired in my left eye and my knees were healed from years of chronic pain and joint popping. The things we had been seeing just happened to me and God's Word was confirmed in my own body. It really revolutionized my thinking and belief structure. We weren't in a church, there had been no worship service to build up to anything, we were eating, and it was for the world to see! It got deep in my spirit, deeper than ever before! I had a confidence that God would confirm His word in ways I had never realized before. It is all about Jesus indeed! When we speak His word, He alone will confirm it!

I was praying for a lady one day in church. During the prayer all I could hear was this other lady behind me saying yes Lord, if it be your will. I was praying God's Word, therefore, I was praying and speaking His will. I stopped and asked the lady to be quiet as I didn't need the hindrance of unbelief during a time of earnest prayer. God's will is for people to be healed from sickness.

Our problem is this, we really don't know whether it is sickness or affliction. There is a very distinct difference in these two.

We were ministering in a Hispanic Church in Gorman, TX in 2002. After the service we held a prayer line for the people. I got to the last person in the line, and I heard the LORD say, don't put your hand on that lady! I couldn't, in my mind rationalize God saying not to pray for somebody. It just didn't make sense to me at all. Since I had rationalized that it was just me and what was going on didn't seem like God to me, I put my hand on the lady's head. Instantly, I felt pain go up my arm and out my shoulder. The only way I can really explain it is, it was like grabbing a live high voltage wire and the voltage going up my arm and out my shoulder. It hurt! I didn't understand yet!

We left there and went to the Hispanic pastor's sisters' house. She called her parents in Mexico, who were also ministers while we were there. Her Mom had been having some health issues and she asked for me to pray for her over the phone. The Lord healed those issues immediately. I thought aside from the pain, nothing was wrong.

The next morning, I was so ill that I could not get out of bed. I laid in that bed asking God for help. I couldn't figure out what had happened to me. I hadn't been ill in a long time. This was weird!

As I sought God on this issue, He took me to His word!

James 13:13-18; *13 Is any among you afflicted? let him pray. Is any merry? let him sing psalms. 14 Is any sick among you? let him call for the elders of the church; and let them pray over him, anointing him with oil in the name of the Lord: 15 And the prayer of faith shall save the sick, and the Lord shall raise him up; and if he have committed sins, they shall be forgiven him. 16 Confess your faults one to another, and pray one for another, that ye may be healed. The effectual fervent prayer of a righteous man availeth much. 17 Elias was a man subject to like passions as we are, and he prayed earnestly that it might not rain: and it rained not on the earth by the space of three years and six months. 18 And he prayed again, and the heaven gave rain, and the earth brought forth her fruit.*

I still didn't understand what He was trying to show me. I began to seek the face of God and try to find what message I needed to learn. Verse 13 asks, is any among you afflicted? Verse 14 asks "is any sick among you?" What? There must be a difference in sickness and affliction! I did some research and a lot of soul searching. God began to reveal to me that affliction is allowed by God to draw a person closer to Him. It is used to bring Glory to God through the hear change of man. God had placed me in a position to learn a lesson. The lesson, I was afflicted for the purpose of learning the things of God a little more clearly.

Jesus gave us dominion over sickness. Sickness is where the enemy has crept in and become a trespasser in one's body. It is for this reason we can command these things to flee, and people will be healed.

My question to God was simply, "How would I know?" He showed me that it is an individual responsibility to seek out the reason for their condition, just as I had done. I repented for putting my hand on that lady's head and immediately, I was well. It was a tough three-day crash course on healing thought and the meaning of a scripture. God says, that after both the beginning of the 13th verse and 14th verse the Word says to "let him" and the actions are given. God says it is this way because only "him" knows the difference. I learned this the hard way.

God went on to reveal to me that the only one that has authority over affliction is HIM! Man was not given that authority. Believers only have authority over sickness. The harsh revelation came with this next statement I received from God: The church and its believers are not suffering from sickness as much as affliction. God wants His church to come close to Him. A good friend and country entertainer, that has gone on to be with the LORD, Johnny Duncan, wrote a song called "Come a Little Bit Closer" That is what God desires for His church.

The lady I had placed my hand on was under affliction and I had overstepped my authority, or at least attempted to. I have been very careful since as to who I place my hand on. I make sure God is working with me as I do, and from there, He will confirm Hid word!

Most people think you have to be some high-powered preacher to see things like this happen.

People are who God uses! He uses anyone that is willing and believes. He says Elijah was a man of like passions and he prayed, and the heavens shut up for seven years and it didn't rain and then he prayed again, and the rain came. We are all geared the same. No sense running to a church, if you're a believer, get to praying and watch God confirm what He says is to be!

Without fail, when we teach this message, we will see someone in need of healing or a miracle. We will ask them to come up front and we will do as the word of God instructs us to do. We will minister to that person and pray for them. Sometimes we ask God for healing but most often, we just call on the mighty and precious name of Jesus to do a miracle in a person's life. Without fail! God Confirms His Word!

Why is this important today? The time is coming when the church will have to not only be the spiritual hospital, but it will have the mission of performing healings and working of miracles. I long maintain the local church should have three crosses on them; one should be red, one should be blue, and one should be green. The Church should be represented as a First

Aid Station. It should be a health care facility and a place of Safety! These are all going to be essential for God's people! The Body of Christ will once again have to be the place people come for real help! It is time to stand up for God and let Him take a stand for you! Don't be surprised what God will use you to do, if you are willing.

We have seen people with terminal cancer healed, we have seen people with heart problems have them removed, we have seen dismal outcomes turn into 30-minute surgeries confusing the doctor, we have seen deaf ears get hearing restored, eyesight restored, knees repaired, rotator cuffs healed, hips healed, ear infections healed, backs straightened out and many more things at the hands of the ministry we do. It is not about us; it is about a God that is so true and loving that He confirms His word!

God Bless you and go into the world and experience God using you!

16 - Signs of Man's Church Versus God's Church

Though we do what we feel is the will of God, we oftentimes get caught up in the religious traditions of the church. People are coming into the church and leaving as fast as they come in. This is because the social club of man, called church is not really doing the true work of God but is engaging in personal standards and goals. This church is a church that brings about bondage instead of the freedom that Jesus came to secure for us as believers of God and Jesus.

The true revelation is this, God's church is doing fine! Man's church is in one big mess!

Let's look at some of the traits of the church as it has regressed and become more of a social club than a place of service and worship.

Paul wrote to young Timothy in:

2 Timothy 4:3-4; *3 For the time will come when they will not endure sound doctrine; but after their own lusts shall they heap to themselves teachers,* *having itching ears; 4 And they shall turn away their ears from the truth and shall be turned unto fables.*

It doesn't take a college graduate to figure out what Paul is telling Timothy. He starts out by telling him to teach the whole truth and the word of God while he can. There are some changes coming to the world that will adversely affect the church. Men will no longer be able to handle the truth of the word of God and will want to listen to things more pleasant to hear. People today, do not really want to know what the true and Living God is about. They have been complacent in how they worship, going to church and getting out at a certain time. They can pretty well do what they want to do. After all, they own the building, and the pastor is their hireling. If he/she doesn't tell us what we want to hear, OUT with Him! And get someone that will make us feel better. Because of this mindset, ministers have compromised and began to soft shoe around the things of God. This takes us to the next scripture that actually is written first by Paul but rightly should follow this scripture. You see, these are the traits that cause the revolving door in the ministry to start spinning.

2 Timothy 3:1-6 *1 This know also, that in the last days perilous times shall come. 2 For men shall be lovers of their own selves, covetous, boasters, proud, blasphemers, disobedient to parents, unthankful, unholy, 3 Without natural affection, trucebreakers, false accusers, incontinent, fierce, despisers of those that are good, 4 Traitors, heady, high-minded, lovers of* *pleasures more than lovers of God; 5 Having a form of godliness, but denying the power thereof: from such turn away. 6 For of this sort are they which creep into houses, and lead captive silly women laden with sins, led away with diverse lusts, 7 Ever learning, and never able to come to the knowledge of the truth.*

In short, the writings of Paul are very direct in what will happen once again. He describes the carnal nature of man over taking the church. The things of the world have crept in and began to dominate the church. The church is getting perverted in what it is teaching to keep people happy. Man will love their selves more than they do God or others. Their word will not be any good. Integrity in lifestyle will disappear. They will begin to resist the things that are good and right. They will go through the motions. They will sing some songs and they will pay some half-hearted homage to the LORD. They will pretend to be Christians while they are there in the church but have a different lifestyle away from the church. They will have that form of godliness but will deny the power thereof.

There are people that make professions of faith and turn their life over to the LORD today and the next time you see a family member they will deny God could have saved that person. What kind of powerless God do they think we serve and takes care of us? These people do not know, nor do they really believe because they are not being taught or don't want to be taught.

It is these people that take silly women captive. The silly women are the church that is not being led by the Holy Ghost. They are being led into captivity and being held in bondage. They do the things that they want to do and demand that God bless them for it. How arrogant is this thought pattern? They will lead a church into the things of the world and get them so bound that ministry cannot be done and the debt becomes the God they are working to serve.

Though things are being taught, they are being taught in error and the truth can never be learned. People can sit in a church for years and until the truth is actually taught, they will not grow, and they can never come to the knowledge of the truth. This knowledge is the true love and grace of God, given to us through Jesus, His Son. It is about how He loved and dealt with people, not how we want to hold to the letter of the law. Leave the judging to the judge and be the student that serves as a teacher at the same time. Be willing to learn and willing to teach others. Jesus sought His Father in Heaven for wisdom and yet He was the teacher. Now we have the benefit of the Holy Ghost to help us. If God wanted us to be anything aside from human beings, He would have had us named Human Doings.

Lamentations 2:14; *Thy prophets have seen vain and foolish things for thee: and they have not* *discovered thine iniquity, to turn away thy captivity; but have seen for thee false burdens and causes of banishment.*

It is significant to note that the same situations existed in the Old Testament as in the New. God is blunt here as He calls these prophets "Thy". You see, they weren't God's prophets at all. Man had called them. Once again, we find that these people were not letting people know what really needed to take place in their lives but rather encouraged them to do things that were not from God.

A study, some years back, done by my friends John Maxwell and Stan Tolar, revealed that if the Holy Ghost were to withdraw His presence from the earth right now, the church would continue to do 95% of what is does and say they were being led by the Holy Ghost. Pretty alarming! A true prophet will be able to minister and get things in your life behind you and let you enjoy the freedom Jesus gave us through His shed Blood on Calvary. The church was not placed on the earth to exchange one form of bondage for another but to rid man of the bondage! This bondage comes in many different forms. If you can think of it, it can be bondage! The old Nike saying, if it feels good do it, doesn't apply to the work of the LORD. Some of the LORD's work feels anything but good.

Lamentations 4:1

1How is the gold become dim! how is the most fine gold changed! the stones of the sanctuary are poured out in the top of every street.

The Temple (church) has lost her beauty! It is pretty much destroyed. The people are the stones that are poured out into the streets. The churches are emptying because people are not getting what they are looking for.

2The precious sons of Zion, comparable to fine gold, how are they esteemed as earthen pitchers, the work of the hands of the potter!

The ministers are looked up to. They are men, created by the LOD. This is the image of the former days when the priesthood was held up and respected.

3Even the sea monsters draw out the breast, they give suck to their young ones: the daughter of my people is become cruel, like the ostriches in the wilderness.

But something has happened whereby the ministers are holding back. The LORD says that even other animals will do whatever to feed their young. Yet, the church has become cruel and refuses to feed the people of God. They are fending for themselves instead of serving others. They are running around taking cover, hiding and ducking from helping God's people.

4The tongue of the sucking child cleaveth to the roof of his mouth for thirst: the young children ask bread, and no man breaketh it unto them.

The young, newly born-again believer is hungry. Like a small child they need milk. They are so thirsty, that their mouth is dry, and their tongue is sticking to the roof of their mouth. There is absolutely nothing fresh entering the body. When they get really hungry and need something solid, people have quit giving any kind of spiritual nourishment to them. God's people are starving to death from lack of feeding.

Amos said there would be a famine in the land, and it would not be a famine of food but of the Word of GOD. Jeremiah is bringing it forth and telling the cause.

5They that did feed delicately are desolate in the streets: they that were brought up in scarlet embrace dunghills.

Those ministers that used to feed the people are out in the streets by themselves. They are pretty much alone. Ministry is a lonely place to be, if you are looking for human acceptance. It is the only place to really be as we walk and live with and in God. These ministers were teaching the Blood of Jesus and His redemptive message. They know the only way to the Father is through the shed blood of a Savior named Jesus. But many have embraced the things of the world as opposed to hanging onto the hope of Salvation through the Blood of Jesus!

153

We are living in a time that we must turn to God with all our heart. We must learn to love the LORD and let that Love of God also flow through us out to others. It is not where people come from in their past. It is about Jesus dying for them as He did for everyone. It is about me, developing the character of Christ in me to love people unconditionally. It is about me growing in the LORD to be able to forgive people as Jesus forgave them and God has forgiven them. It is up to me to be able to leave the past alone and help people today and into the future. Some things people have been through are just really none of our business. If we hear it from them, we should learn to not gossip but keep it to our self.

God allows the local assembly the opportunity to come into agreement with Him on a pastor for the church. He allows them to feel they call the pastor. Jeremiah is pretty plain about the fact that God sends the pastor (shepherds) He wants us to have. Laugh and humor yourselves as you weigh this against the Word of God. God has control of His church. He will bring it to where He wants her. We are the Body of Christ and His presence in the community! That being the case, we should strive to be imitators of Jesus, as He leads, not as religion dictates. If we do these things and guard against the prior, we will surely learn and grow to live victorious in all things. The church is God's, and we should respond to the head, Christ Jesus. We should be open to the truth and be willing to accept it, even if we first take offense. I have heard things plenty of times and had to go back, get into prayer and seek God for the answer. 99% of the time, I will get the answer from God about what I heard was from Him and He adjusted part of my belief structure through it.

You are children of God! You are who you are because of who's you are! God has a great plan for you and wants the very best for you. Stand up for God and He will stand for you! Get uncomfortable and grew from the discomfort. It will glorify God and bring a new Joy to your life.

17 - The Truth About Abortion

1 Timothy 6:3-11

Introduction: In recent weeks we have been watching the elected officials boldly step into the limelight and flaunt legislation in the face of the true believers while simultaneously shaking their fist in the face of our Very HOLY God. The Lord had it penned for us; it is a dangerous thing to fall into the hands of an ANGRY God. Not only have many of the elected servants of this country fallen into the hands of God, but they also jumped in, daring Him to do something.

I for one spoke out against the stance of the church, and namely the Catholic Church for not openly taking a stand and excommunicating the Governor of New York. The Catholic Church has a stronger platform on which to stand and speak out to make a person a public shame through excommunication. In speaking to the Archbishop of the Mexican National Catholic Church, I have learned, there is a provision under the Code of Cannon Law, which governs the Catholic Church, referred to as "Ispo Facto" (by that very fact or act : as an inevitable result) whereby offenders in effect excommunicate themselves from such actions. Who knows what the church will do, but they have handed the enemy a lot of power in not standing up.

If you care to, turn in your Bible to 1 Timothy 5:20,

"Them that sin rebuke before all, that others also may fear." In accordance with God's Word, there should be a public rebuke and action against them. We could go to Titus 3:10 which actually speaks to the removal of a person from the congregation or Body of Christ for the purpose of assembly.

Sad to say, Catholics were not the only group involved in this act. There are many other people who attend Protestant Churches who were involved in passing this law. Well known politicians were avid supporters and were there when the bill was signed and they profess to be a Christian, however their actions point to them just being witches.

Now, following the state of NY, VA, CT and DE are all jumping on the bandwagon of late term abortion. This is murder, plain and simple. Abortion is NEVER good! Now, if there is a botched abortion, as the baby is being delivered and they are still alive, they can be placed aside, denied medical assistance and left to die. Church, that is infanticide!

Here is why abortion is so promoted: hear these figures:

$22,610 Brain

$7,140   Heart

$2,975   Liver

$2,670   Limbs

$7,140   Pancreas

$42,535 = Total for Body Parts.

NOW, let's see what this really boils down to, according to the Word of God:

1 Timothy 6: *3 If any man teach otherwise, and consent not to wholesome words, even the words of our Lord Jesus Christ, and to the doctrine which is according to godliness;*

4 He is proud, knowing nothing, but doting about questions and strifes of words (angry or bitter disagreement over fundamental issues; conflict), whereof cometh envy (desire to have a quality, possession, or other desirable attribute belonging to (someone else), strife, railings (complain or protest strongly and persistently about), evil surmisings (suppose that something is true without having evidence to confirm it),

5 Perverse (showing a deliberate and obstinate desire to behave in a way that is unreasonable or unacceptable, often in spite of the consequences) disputings (argue about (something); discuss heatedly) of men of corrupt (cause to act dishonestly in return for money or personal gain, bribe · suborn · buy · buy off · pay off

), minds, and destitute (devoid · bereft · deprived · in need · bankrupt · empty · drained · exhausted · depleted · bare · denuded · lacking · without · deficient in · wanting) of the truth (JESUS: John 14:6, I AM the Way, the Truth and the Life!") , supposing that gain is godliness: from such withdraw thyself.

6 But godliness with contentment (state of happiness and satisfaction.) is great gain.

7 For we brought nothing into this world, and it is certain we can carry nothing out.

8 And having food and raiment let us be therewith content (state of satisfaction).

9 But they that will be rich (having a great deal of money or assets; wealthy) fall into temptation and a snare (trap), and into many foolish and hurtful lusts, (very strong intimate desire), which drown men in destruction and perdition (a state of eternal punishment and damnation into which a sinful and impenitent (unrepentant) person passes after death).

*10 For **the love (**an intense feeling of deep affection) **of money** is the root of all evil: which while some coveted after, they have erred from the faith, and pierced themselves through with many sorrows.*

11 But thou, O man of God, flee these things; and follow after righteousness, godliness, faith, love, patience, meekness.

2 Timothy 3: 3 This know also, that in the last days perilous (full of danger or risk) times shall come. Today it is a dangerous time to be an unborn child and its mother. There is no real care about the mother. This is not about women's rights; this is about greed! This is about sacrifice to a false God. It is a blood sacrifice and is every form of witchcraft.

2 For men shall be lovers of their own selves, covetous (having or showing a great desire to possess something belonging to someone else), boasters (an act of talking with excessive pride and self-satisfaction), proud (having or showing a high or excessively high opinion of oneself or one's importance), blasphemers (speak irreverently about God or sacred things), disobedient (refusing to obey rules or someone in authority) to parents, unthankful (unappreciative · unthankful · thankless · ungracious), unholy (sinful; wicked),

3 Without natural (any person or thing that is or is likely or certain to be very suitable to and successful in an endeavor without much training or difficulty) affection (a gentle feeling of fondness or liking), trucebreakers (one who violates a truce, covenant, or engagement), false accusers, incontinent (lacking self-restraint; uncontrolled), fierce (having or displaying an intense or ferocious aggressiveness), despisers (feel contempt or a deep repugnance for) of those that are good,

[4] Traitors (person who betrays a friend, country, principle, etc.), heady (potent; intoxicating), high-minded (upliftedness in a bad sense, pride, arrogance), lovers of pleasures more than lovers of God;

[5] Having a form of godliness, but denying the power thereof: from such turn away.

[6] For of this sort are they which creep into houses, and lead captive silly women laden (heavily loaded or weighed down) with sins, led away with divers (varying types; several) lusts (very strong intimate desire),

[7] Ever learning, and never able to come to the knowledge of the truth.

[8] Now as Jannes and Jambres (the 2 magicians in the Pharaoh's court that came against Moses) withstood Moses, so do these also resist the truth: men of corrupt (cause to act dishonestly in return for money or personal gain) minds, reprobate (an unprincipled person) concerning the faith.

[9] But they shall proceed no further: for their folly shall be manifest unto all men, as theirs's also was.

You can see by all what the Lord has to say in this Scripture, this is all about man and his lack of relationship with Him. Mankind turns to whatever they desire and forget what God desires, especially, as it seems to benefit them more or maybe more quickly. They are considered enemies in the language used. He calls them "Traitors." This is what draws out the greed! He says; "the LOVE of money" is the root of all evil. It is money they are after at the expense of the mother and child. These folks do not care about either one involved in the procedure, just the financial gain.

Here is the spiritual condition in which they walk and live.

Galatians 5: *16 This I say then, Walk in the Spirit, and ye shall not fulfil the lust of the flesh.*

17 For the flesh lusteth against the Spirit, and the Spirit against the flesh: and these are contrary (cannot work together) the one to the other: so that ye cannot do the things that ye would.

18 But if ye be led of the Spirit, ye are not under the law.

19 Now the works of the flesh are manifest, which are these; Adultery, fornication, uncleanness (morally wrong), lasciviousness (revealing an overt and often offensive sexual desire),

20 Idolatry (extreme admiration, love, or reverence for something or someone), witchcraft (the practice of and belief in magical skills), hatred (intense dislike or ill will), variance (a discrepancy between two statements or documents), emulations (effort to match or surpass a person or achievement), wrath (extreme anger), strife (angry or bitter disagreement over fundamental issues; conflict), seditions (overt conduct, such as speech and organization, that tends toward insurrection against the established order), heresies (belief or opinion contrary to orthodox religious (especially Christian) doctrine), envyings, murders, drunkenness, revellings (enjoy oneself in a lively and noisy way, especially with drinking and dancing), and such like: of the which I tell you before, as I have also told you in time past, that they which do such things shall not inherit (come into possession of (something) as a right) the kingdom of God.

Conclusion: We have all these scriptures speaking to us about the condition of the human heart of people who have gotten away from the Lord or have never been with Him at all. Some of these folks are in church today and they give to the church they go to but, they still are caught up in the delusion the enemy has placed before them. Oftentimes, people are caught up in the situation in ways they do not realize they are caught up. Being silent is to be complacent of the sin. Some would argue the Governor may not have had a choice, he could have been overridden. Then let the majority override him to keep his hands clean. Then, once these things pass, the attack by and on Christian begin to intensify.

There are ruthless attacks made against the people of God who stand against these things. Many have spoken out saying that abortion is not a bad procedure. I am convinced; Abortion has allowed the world to view human life from a different lens. A lens that allows human life to be exterminated by one person whenever they feel that another person is no

164

longer valuable. Abortion unleashed a spirit of murder across this country. That spirit has led to greed by selling body parts. And as you, the Christian stands up, you come under persecution. So, let me end in the words of our Savior by reading:

John 16: *16 These things have I spoken unto you, that ye should not be offended.*

2 They shall put you out of the synagogues: yea, the time cometh, that whosoever killeth you will think that he doeth God service.

3 And these things will they do unto you, because they have not known the Father, nor me.

Verse 3 is the bottom line in this whole issue. Abortion is a Spiritual problem! We, as a church, we as a Christian assembly, we as the Body of Christ need to pray for the conversion of these people and for God to be all He is in their lives, be it in mercy or Righteous Judgment. We cannot sit still!

18 - Walk of Transformation

We enter into this life from a spiritual being to that of a physical being. At some point in the physical stage of life, we are awakened to the plan God has for us by a move of the Holy Ghost. From that day forward, we begin walking with God or chasing after Him and His ways until we are able to return to the place in which we originated. (Jeremiah 1:5, Isaiah 49:1, Ephesians 1:4 and John 15:26-27)

Genesis 5:21-24; *And Enoch lived sixty and five years, and begat Methuselah. 22) And Enoch walked with God after he begat Methuselah three hundred years, and begat sons and daughters. 23) And all the days of Enoch were three hundred sixty and five years: 24) And Enoch walked with God and he was not; for God took him.*

(This section of the scriptures also captures that Enoch had the shortest lifespan in the account of the 5th chapter of Genesis)

Enoch was at the 65th year of his life when an event took place. In this case it was the birth of Methuselah. This event marks the day that Enoch started his quest in chasing God. Our common versions of the Bible show this account as Enoch "walked" with God. The version differs from the actual Hebrew translation which actually has a direct interpretation to the word "chase" or "to chase" as in "chasing after." This change in life caused Enoch to do something he hadn't been doing for the first 65 years of his life and that was being a "God chaser". In today's teachings and understanding of theology, we would call this what John Wesley refers to as the awakening process, wrought on by the Holy Spirit to draw us into a reconciled relationship with God. We would also refer to it as the point in life that one would say they have experienced a crisis that brought about a mind change (repentance) which caused them to acknowledge Christ as Lord and Savior in their life. Enoch began this walk with God or this persistent chase after God that went the remainder of his life. It was imperative in this chase after God that Enoch had the willingness to be obedient to the things God spoke to him. God had Amos to write this scripture that must be applied to everybody walking with God or chasing after God in life. Amos 3:3; "Can two walk together, except they be agreed?" Enoch and God must have agreed on much since they were together for 300 years. Can I say they always agreed on everything? No! Can I say they never had a discussion on differences? No! But the scripture is clear, 300 years this relationship carried forth. In the development of a relationship, we find we can openly speak of more and more things that we don't understand or really have our own understanding of. As we step into the relationship building part of our walk, this is the 300-year span of time representing Enoch's life with chasing God or as we would refer to it today as serving God with all our heart.

Relationships are built on time and plenty of it. You can meet somebody today and know them but know nothing about them. You may get to know a little about someone but, that still doesn't develop a friendship or strong relationship. Relationship is something that is both individual and unique. It is something that is tailor made to fit the people involved. It is a bond that allows us to see past one's faults to the perfection in someone. It is developed on two factors, love and trust. Sometimes we don't have to understand, we just have to love the other person. Let's take a look at the next scriptures as we fill in the time of 300 years in Enoch's life.

Romans 12:1-3; *"I beseech you therefore brethren, by the mercies of God, that you present your bodies as a living sacrifice, holy, acceptable unto God, which is your reasonable service. 2) And be not conformed to the things of this world; but be ye transformed by the renewing of your mind, that ye may prove what is that good and acceptable, and perfect will of God. 3) For I say, through the grace given unto me, to every man that is among you, not to think of himself more highly than he ought to think; but to think soberly, according as God has dealt to every man the measure of faith."*

As Enoch walked with God for these 300 years, there was much that would have to transpire for Enoch to build his relationship with God. Maybe not as we would think in our mind, but God was getting to know Enoch, not like he didn't already, since He created him but more importantly Enoch was getting to know God.

As we come to the awakening in our life and become repentant, born-again believers, we to begin to learn more and more about the God we serve. The more we learn about Him, the more we love Him, the more we understand what He desires for us to be, and the less apt we are to deliberately do anything to hurt God's feelings. We want God to be able to trust us too! We want to model our self after Jesus who is the Christ!

I have found in my personal life, the closer I got to people, the less I was apt to do that would bring harm or embarrassment to them. In fact, the opposite really takes place, I have found myself working to protect people and standing in the gap for them. This is the transformation of the mind. It is when you or I think less of ourselves and more of others. It is when we are willing to sacrifice for others whatever it takes to help them.

God doesn't call us or ask us to do things that will hurt us but rather help Him be glorified. If the outcome is that everybody gets hurt, then it probably should not be done. The outcome of all we do should ultimately point towards Jesus.

This transformation is a lifetime effort. For Enoch it took 300 years. Life spans are considerably shorter now than then, but we still have a span of time to walk or chase after God in our life. We have a space of time to repent before this walk begins and that happens when God sends out the call.

Some years back, we were helping a congressman's widow campaign for congress in the next election following her husband's tragic death in a plane crash. She was sharing with us that her husband had flown to Hattiesburg, MS to throw out the first pitch for the Little League World's Series. He was wearing a light blue suite with a dark blue shirt that night. On the way home, the plane was not on the course it was supposed to be on, reasons not really known, and the plane crashed in the DeSoto National Forest killing her husband and the pilot. She had the people on the rescue team take her to the crash site. As she was talking to the Lord about her husband and what had happened, she had a butterfly come and land on her arm and fluttered its wings then flew off. The butterfly was light blue with a dark blue trim around it. She said peace came over her as the Lord told her that his transformation was now complete.

Since the word transformation comes from the Greek word, we get the word Metamorphosis and it really relates to the transformation of the caterpillar through the cocoon stage to the final stage of a beautiful butterfly, this account really spoke to me.

As people develop relationships with God through their chasing of Him, they are going through this transformation process. It is God's design for man to be all they can be in eternal beauty. We do not see anybody instructing Enoch in this relationship building time with God. It was about him and God. In the individual development of a butterfly in its transformation process, if we pull a butterfly loose from the cocoon before the final cord or attachment is cut, we will damage or kill the butterfly before transformation is completed. So, it is with the development of people in a personal relationship with God. If we are not careful, we can pull them loose from the very thing that is giving them life and destroy them or kill them spiritually. This account of Enoch shows the importance of personal relationship building and alone time with God.

Of course, Enoch walked with or chased God for 300 years. I believe it would be a safe bet to say not many of us will have to work so long in reaching the next step that Enoch moved to.

19 - We've Got Work to Do!

Revelation 7:9; *"After this I beheld, and, lo, a great multitude, which no man could number, of all nations, and kindreds and people, and tongues, stood before the throne, and before the Lamb, clothed with white robes, and palms in their hands:"*

One day, as I read through the Word of God, I was drawn to Revelation 7:9. It says that around the throne were gathered people of every tribe, nation, and kingdom, to big in number to count. Reality hit me between the eyes as I realized I was looking at a picture of the raptured church. I was overwhelmed with the thought that, man, we've got some serious work to do!

Jesus gave us the Great Commission in Matthew 28. We know that the fall of man caused us to be born into a state of sin. Just how do we express that fall? In October 2002, Cheryl and I had the privilege of being at the Billy Graham School of Evangelism in the Metroplex in the Dallas area. It was a great week spent with people who today are real spiritual giants. We saw and heard men of God that we had only listened to on the radio. We heard them tell how God was directing their ministries and how He had blessed them. On the Thursday night meeting of the crusade, we went into the Texas stadium to see Dr Graham deliver God's message. It was not like any other stadium I had ever been in. We walked out on the stairway and proceeded down the steps. Well, I was joking with some guys behind me about all good Baptists would have to sit up front that night. There was a big blue tarp covering the playing field, a long way below. As I turned to look for the next step, I missed it in the line of my bi-focals and began to fall forward. My wife was right in front of me, so naturally, I reached for her.

Although I know she loves me dearly, she hurriedly moved so as not to be knocked over by my fall. I was going face first down these stairs not knowing where I was going to stop. When I finally stopped, it was in front of all the ministers that had been teaching us that day. As I got up, people ask me was I okay? My response was yes. My wife just took off across the front of the stadium seats and then decided to climb over a row to sit near some of the friends we had made there. (This school and crusade were real treats for us as we had managed somehow to bump the announcement that Billy Graham was coming to Texas to the bottom of the page of the December 31, 2001 Baptist Standard, as God gave us the first three quarters of the page in a newspaper with about 150,000 in circulation.) We never thought we would be on the same page with Billy Graham let alone be in a place to hear him speak. I had sprained my right wrist and my left ankle. This combination made it nearly impossible to do anything. The crusade was great, and we really enjoyed the word of the Lord delivered through Dr Graham. What I learned about all this was, the fall of man was not a flat on the face kind of fall. This fall is one that is gradual that will only stop at the pits of hell unless we answer the tug in our heart from the Lord. The distance that people fall is different from each other, but the separation and the ultimate destiny could be the same. It was then that I realized that even those around us sidestep us during the fall we encounter and will walk off and leave us once we stop. As I said, my wife loves me dearly. I am convinced that she wouldn't want to see any harm done to me unless it was going to hurt her too! Is this the way it works? I was thinking that we so often are willing to stand until it might affect us, then we step out of the way. There is much uncertainty involved in the fall. Yes, my wife was there when my fall stopped. She asked the same question all people ask when someone has a mishap. Are you all right? No! I wasn't all right, but my pride wouldn't let me say that I was messed up. I surely didn't want to let anyone know that I was physically hurting; after all, I was already embarrassed pretty bad. Maybe I suffered through some things I didn't need to suffer through as a result of my pride in refusing to admit I was hurt. I didn't want sympathy, but I didn't anticipate climbing over chair rows either. I believe we are quick in asking if someone is hurt and when they respond with a no, we abandon them to fend for themselves. They are wounded and very vulnerable to falling again. Once a person gets up from this fall, it is up to us to help them to become spiritually well once again. This fall was not about my wife or my clowning, it was about God showing me that man is falling in a sloping downward trend with the bottom stop being Hell itself. We can, through our own testimony serve as a step to stop the downhill slide of someone that is sliding into Hell. The key is, in order to have a Testimony; you must first endure the test!

As we are going to be gathered around the Throne of Jesus, we will be worshipping Him throughout all eternity. We will all be together worshipping the only true and Living God, our Savior and Lord, Jesus Christ. Do you think that we will be hurting then? I think not! There is not going to be any kind of separation from God because of socio-economic or cultural barriers, which man has imposed. It will be all about serving Jesus. I am reminded when Jesus spoke to the scribes that there was virtue in the room to heal them all but only the paralytic lowered through the roof was healed because of faith.

We have a good friend that is a songwriter. He had written a song some years back but was able to have it recorded recently on a new CD from the Oak Ridge Boys. Rock Killough, from Greenville, Alabama wrote and sang about the problems of this world and playing the blame game with who is at fault. The bottom line to the song is, we are in trouble because of the "Absence of Love." Thanks to God and to Rock Killough for this song. Thanks to the Oaks for singing it and putting it out for the world to hear. What better time could we be hearing such a song? Our united praises to God should be started right here on earth. Oh, for the desire to see man love one another. Jesus said that we should love one another as He has loved us. Rock has also written another song that unlocks the door to every emotion we could ever have. Rock writes: "You've got to get the Love of Jesus in your heart." It is essential that we find and get this love and share it, without reservation, and become witnesses for Christ.

20 - Integrity - Missing Ingredient in Walking With God

Psalm 26:1-3; *"Judge me, O LORD; for I have walked in mine integrity: I have trusted also in the LORD; therefore, I shall not slide. Examine me, O LORD; and prove me; try my reins and my heart. For thy loving kindness is before mine eyes; and I have walked in thy truth."*

David was speaking to the LORD about something in his life. This something was integrity. David says that he walked in his own integrity and asked God to see if it measured up. He was so confident in his relationship and leading from God that he was not the least bit concerned regarding how things would stack up. He says his trust was in God and that he was confident he would not have any troubles.

My heart's desire is that ministers and believers across the world would make this same cry to God. A cry that asks if they measure up to the standard God has given us in Christ. What is lacking severely from the ministry and the church today is this ingredient of integrity. One's integrity comes into play the moment

179

that turbulence arrives. Ministers that fall from grace are usually damaged by issues of integrity.

David says that he was "blameless" a word that has been redefined from its original meaning. Today a person is blameless if they have not been accused. The original meaning of the word is to be accused or blamed without fault. In other words, many people are blamed that haven't done anything wrong. Jesus was blamed, but even Pilate, after hearing the accusation, said he found no fault with Him. Yet, due to man's rebellion, Jesus was wrong in their eyes, and they would stop at nothing less than death to prevent the "right" from going forth. They were following accusation!

It is important that we strive to be "blameless" and upright before both God and man. It is important that we, as believers and ministers, do the things we commit and promise to do. If we give our word and then don't follow through, we are no longer blameless. We can be accused with fault. David was concerned enough about this that he cried out to God to inspect him. David went a step further and asked God to examine his integrity. We too should be willing to allow God to expose the motives of our heart in the things we do. It is easy to say the right thing, but then be plotting something totally different in your mind. Would you be willing to let God expose this to you and above all, would you be willing for God to expose these things to all of mankind? Can we walk in this and be ok? Our integrity cannot stack up to Christ, but through the Blood of Jesus, we have been made whole and can stand but only by the Grace of God.

Many times, things come to us that challenge our integrity as we decide what to do or how to respond. Our integrity is tried, and our heart pulled as we grow in this area. Many ministers walk in an aura of arrogance feeling they have no responsibility to anybody but God. We are accountable to God for what we do, but we are also responsible to our flock for how we minister to them. The integrity that David was ensuring he had, if missing, is the very thing that has caused many a ministry to fail and many believers to be damaged. God cannot lie and since we are supposed to be like Him, how can we profess to be like Him and miss this key ingredient? David didn't want to miss it nor do I.

Lord help me to be more like Jesus and walk in a greater level of integrity.

What is Integrity? Well, it really means that we should walk, as best as possible, in the likeness of Christ. David said he didn't hang out with evil doers and wicked people. He knew that doing so would transform his walk into something less than what the LORD desires from us. There are many things that show a lack of integrity in the ministry and the church. Such as living a life that is a lie, your word being no good, your actions not reflecting your speech, and not following through on your obligations and promises.

Some years ago, we were in a service business. If we quoted someone a price to do a job, we didn't exceed that cost because we had already told the people what it would be. If we exceeded our costs, we absorbed the extra. If the completed job came in below our estimate, we would give them the lower price, if possible. Financially, it cost us from time to time, but relationally, it developed good customers and good friends who knew they could trust us. We try to operate in the ministry in the same manner. We give it our best to give all we can, even at a personal cost because we have realized there is much gain in personal sacrifice.

David could see God's lovingkindness and anyone that chooses to walk with God in a walk of integrity will see his lovingkindness. God will take care of you. While it may seem easier sometimes to tell something that is not entirely true to get through a situation, the truth is that you will always be found out and then it becomes harder. The truth is always the best way out and I try to stand on it at any cost. Sometimes it is not comfortable for us, but it is always best. The man that taught me my trade in auto mechanics used to tell me that, "if a man lies to you, he will steal from you as well." Your flock feels the same way about you.

David had his problems and since none of us are perfect, we will have them as well. Spiritual snipers that feel they are superior to you will set up an ambush and attempt to shoot you and knock you down. They will do their best to destroy you even as the LORD is using you. Stay "Blameless" in your walk and watch God's loving kindness cover you as you walk. Walk in the truth of God as David walked.

Finally, the truth that David walked in is unlike the truth we are afforded the privilege of walking in. The truth we walk in is not a what but a person. That person is Christ! We, like David need to walk in that truth. When we walk in TRUTH, (Jesus) we will love people enough to tell them the truth and trust them.

My prayer is for ministers all over the world to experience the integrity that David sought, and that Christ opened for us. Ministers, operating without integrity, have hid behind the cloak of their ministry, and damaged their flocks by their examples and actions. It would be good to see ministers walk in the ways of God and do the things David did or didn't do. David was searching as he speaks about them in Psalm 26. If the church will restore its integrity from the floor up, it will again not only be able to trust people but will begin to love and accept each other and be restored to a glory greater than her former glory.

God Bless you! May this word speak to your heart.

Meet the Author

Randy Heddings

Randy's salvation experience took place at a small Baptist Church in Prichard, AL in June 1974. In 1999, Randy, his wife, and his 12-year-old daughter took off for central Texas to fill an associate pastor's position. In May 2001, they moved to Comanche, TX to work as church planters. To date, they have been instrumental in 35 church plants across Texas and Mississippi. They are also the founding ministers of Job's Place Ministries.

Randy was raised in Ocean Springs, MS, served in the US Army, retired as a Civil Service employee, and currently serves as a government contractor in Pascagoula, MS. Randy holds a BA in Theology from Grace Valley Theological Seminary, a Master of Divinity from Woolsey Hall School of Theology, Oxford, England, a Doctor of Ministry from Grace Valley Theological Seminary, a Theological Doctorate from Grace Valley Theological Seminary and a Doctor of Divinity from Woolsey Hall School of Theology, Oxford England. Randy also holds a BBA and MBA from Concordia College in Logistics Management.